PRAISE FOR *CAN WE TALK?*

Everything you need to know about communication and relationship building at work is right here! Solid insights and practical advice from one of the world's leading authorities on executive coaching and employee engagement.
Marshall Goldsmith, *New York Times* #1 bestselling author of *Triggers*, *Mojo*, and *What Got You Here Won't Get You There*

Who doesn't cringe when they hear the words "Can we talk"? And yet the truth is, those conversations we'd prefer to avoid are essential. I love how Roberta Chinsky Matuson clearly guides us through the process of finding our voice so we can say what most needs to be said. This book is invaluable for leaders—or for anyone who works.
Sally Helgesen, author of *How Women Rise*, *The Female Vision*, and *The Web of Inclusion*

If you want to keep your employees, then you've got to get them talking. Roberta Chinsky Matuson's book will do just that. With memorable stories and examples—including the author's own firsthand experiences of difficult conversations quickly going south—*Can We Talk?* provides readers with tools to actively build better relationships up, down, and across the organization.
Dr. Beverly Kaye, co-author of *Love 'Em or Lose 'Em* and *Up Is Not the Only Way*

There's nothing more important in business than the ability to communicate effectively with those above, below, and across from you. In *Can We Talk?*, Roberta Chinsky Matuson provides readers with a game-changing framework to help them safely navigate through any tough work conversation, while successfully building strong relationships along the way.
Laura Huang, international bestselling author of *Edge* and professor at Harvard Business School

If you've been holding back from saying what needs to be said at work, *Can We Talk?* is the book for you. No topic is off the table here. This is a must-read for business owners, leaders, and employees looking to find their voice and power up their communication skills.
Dorie Clark, author of *Reinventing You* and executive education faculty at Duke University Fuqua School of Business

One of our six core values at Saxbys is "Care Personally and Communicate Openly"—simply because we know how critical, yet difficult, human communication can be. Roberta Chinsky Matuson's book does a fantastic job identifying both the importance of actually having difficult conversations while also providing the guidance to have them effectively.
Nick Bayer, Founder and CEO, Saxbys

This book is essential reading for anyone looking to improve their work relationships and build trust through more effective communication. *Can We Talk?* is one of those books that you'll refer to time and time again.
Jenn Mann, Chief Human Resources Officer, SAS

Can We Talk? is a fast-pass framework to help you move past one-sided conversations, better your career, and achieve a more humanistic workplace.
Marlene Chism, author of *From Conflict to Courage*

Where was *Can We Talk?* when I needed it most? All those well-meaning but frequently awkward conversations that could have been better for all if I had read this. Roberta Chinsky Matuson proves once again that she is the subject matter expert.
Julie Kahn, President, Regan Communications

Roberta Chinsky Matuson has done it again! I find myself wishing I'd had this book when I was a new professional. Matuson's practical approach and no-nonsense language makes this the playbook for improving employee performance. Her planned approach is sure to make giving tough messages a lot easier—and that is the first step to ensuring your employees are exceeding your expectations.
Jay Hargis, First Vice President, Learning and Development Officer, Apple Bank

Can We Talk? gives managers and individual contributors a comprehensive toolbox on how to handle difficult conversations in a productive and constructive manner and elevate performance and employee engagement. It's a must-read for anyone who wants to be successful in their career.
Polina Ware, PhD, Global R&D/TS&D Director, Rogers Corporation

Can We Talk?

Seven Principles for Managing Difficult Conversations at Work

Roberta Chinsky Matuson

KoganPage

First published in Great Britain and the United States in 2022 by Kogan Page Limited

Apart from any fair dealing for the purposes of research or private study, or criticism or review, as permitted under the Copyright, Designs and Patents Act 1988, this publication may only be reproduced, stored or transmitted, in any form or by any means, with the prior permission in writing of the publishers, or in the case of reprographic reproduction in accordance with the terms and licences issued by the CLA. Enquiries concerning reproduction outside these terms should be sent to the publishers at the undermentioned addresses:

2nd Floor, 45 Gee Street
London
EC1V 3RS
United Kingdom
www.koganpage.com

122 W 27th St, 10th Floor
New York, NY 10001
USA

4737/23 Ansari Road
Daryaganj
New Delhi 110002
India

Kogan Page books are printed on paper from sustainable forests.

© Roberta Chinsky Matuson, 2022

ISBNs
Hardback   978 1 3986 0133 8
Paperback   978 1 3986 0130 7
Ebook   978 1 3986 0131 4

British Library Cataloguing-in-Publication Data

A CIP record for this book is available from the British Library.

Library of Congress Cataloging-in-Publication Data

Names: Matuson, Roberta Chinsky, author.
Title: Can we talk?: seven principles for managing difficult conversations
   at work / Roberta Chinsky Matuson.
Description: London; New York, NY: Kogan Page, 2021. | Includes
   bibliographical references and index.
Identifiers: LCCN 2021019090 (print) | LCCN 2021019091 (ebook) | ISBN
   9781398601338 (hardback) | ISBN 9781398601307 (paperback) | ISBN
   9781398601314 (ebook)
Subjects: LCSH: Communication in management. | Interpersonal conflict. |
   Personnel management.
Classification: LCC HD30.3 .M3789 2021 (print) | LCC HD30.3 (ebook) | DDC
   658.4/5–dc23
LC record available at https://lccn.loc.gov/2021019090
LC ebook record available at https://lccn.loc.gov/2021019091

Typeset by Hong Kong FIVE Workshop, Hong Kong
Print production managed by Jellyfish
Printed and bound by CPI Group (UK) Ltd, Croydon CR0 4YY

To my husband, Ron, who has willingly
(and sometimes unwillingly) said "Yes"
whenever I've started a conversation with,
"Can we talk?"
Your support in writing this book means the world to me.
And to our children, Zachary and Lexi.
I hope this book will guide you safely through
the many difficult work conversations you may encounter
as you begin your journey into the world of work.
Lastly, this book is for my late mom, Jeanette,
who gave me the gift of gab.

CONTENTS

ABOUT THE AUTHOR

For more than twenty-five years, Roberta Matuson, president of Matuson Consulting, has helped leaders in highly regarded companies, including General Motors, Takeda, and Microsoft, and small- to medium-size businesses, achieve dramatic growth and market leadership through the maximization of talent.

She's the author of five books, including *Evergreen Talent: How to Seed, Cultivate, and Grow a Sustainable Workforce* and the international bestseller *Suddenly in Charge: Managing Up, Managing Down, Succeeding All Around*, a *Washington Post* Top 5 Business Book for Leaders.

Roberta is also a LinkedIn Top Voice in Workplace and Leadership and the author of seven LinkedIn Learning courses. Her courses can also be found on Skillsoft, MentorBox, and Knowable.

Roberta is one of a handful of people who have appeared as a guest of Bill O'Reilly on Fox's *O'Reilly Factor* and who left the show unscathed.

You can reach out directly to Roberta Matuson at Roberta@robertamatuson.com. Connect with her on LinkedIn and follow her on Twitter @matuson.

ACKNOWLEDGMENTS

This book would not have been possible without the support of my agent, Linda Konner, who worked her magic to secure a book deal on my behalf during a pandemic. I'm incredibly grateful for your tenacity.

Thank you to my editors, Kathe Sweeny and Heather Wood, who helped shape this book, and the staff at Kogan Page. Your suggestions and encouragement along the way were greatly appreciated.

I'd also like to acknowledge my mentor, Alan Weiss, whose guidance has served me well over the years. Your constant push for me to think bigger has resulted in the completion of book number six.

Lastly, a big thank you also goes out to my colleagues, Hugh Blane, Gail Bower, Graham Binks, Noah Fleming, and Lisa Larter. I listen way more than you may think and am grateful for your advice and friendship.

Introduction

The Seven Principles for Managing Difficult Conversations

How Did We Get Here?

The year was 1993, and the day started like any other. I commuted into downtown Boston and rode the elevator up to my office, ready to face a new workweek. Little did I know, that on this day my life was about to change. Before going into more detail here, let me set the stage for what I thought for sure was a dream—well, more like a nightmare.

Back in the early '90s, I was stuck in a job that I didn't love and worked for a boss who made the fictional character of mean boss Miranda Priestly, played by Meryl Steep in the movie *The Devil Wears Prada*, look like an angel. In fact, I'm reasonably sure that Streep spent a few days with my boss getting her moves down.

Admittedly, my relationship with my manager got off to a rocky start. You see, I was hired by her predecessor who left shortly after I started. At that time, I didn't give much thought to the changing of the guard, as bosses are a lot like trains. One pulls into the station, sits for a while, departs, and another one arrives soon thereafter.

From day one, my new boss and I didn't see eye-to-eye on much, making it extremely hard to be successful in my role. She wasn't the type to mince words. She rarely said anything. She didn't need to, as you could usually tell what she was thinking by looking at her frowning face.

I spent a year of my life doing somersaults trying to please her. I honestly thought I was making progress until that fateful day when my boss stopped by my office and said those three words no one wants to hear. "Can we talk?" followed by "Come see me in my office."

My boss then exited as quickly as she had arrived, which was a good thing, as I didn't want her to hear my heart sinking to the bottom of my stomach. I did my best to pull myself together before taking a seat in her office.

Here's how that "conversation" went.

Boss: You're not meeting my expectations (followed by a brief pause). Although, I'm not sure I ever told you what they are.

Me: (looking dumbfounded): Okay.

While all the while, I was thinking, "What the heck?"

She then went on to share what her expectations were, as well as everything I was doing wrong. I sat in shock and kept thinking, "How could I possibly know what her expectations were if she never told me? She went to Harvard. Maybe they taught mind reading there. I attended Northeastern University, where Mind Reading 101 was not a college class offered."

I may have been confused by what my boss had just said. However, I was very clear about one thing. This was the beginning of the end of my time with the organization.

Our time together could have ended very differently, had my boss read an advance copy of *Can We Talk? Seven Principles for Managing Difficult Conversations at Work*. But then again, I might never have written this book had she done so.

I wish I could tell you that this awkward conversation was the only one I experienced throughout my career. Unfortunately, there were plenty more, which I'll be sharing throughout this book.

Crazy encounters, like the one I described, are still taking place in workplaces across the globe and even in outer space (more about that later.) I'm on a mission to make sure what happened to me doesn't happen to you or anyone else you know.

Too many work conversations are one-sided. They're more like a monologue than a dialogue. This has to change if we are ever going to get to a place where we can achieve better outcomes and a more humane workplace.

I'm writing this book because I don't want others to go through what I experienced. I was young (well, maybe not *that* young) and didn't realize that I was giving my power away by sitting there and failing to respond. Power is a funny thing. Once you give it away, it's hard to get back.

Throughout this book, I'll encourage those of you on the receiving end of a difficult work conversation to embrace what may come your way. If you do so and participate from a place of good intent, you'll experience rapid personal growth. Some of the most challenging experiences often result in the most amazing transformations, which is partially what this book is about.

We have a lot of work ahead of us to get to the place where we can regularly have meaningful *and* effective conversations in the workplace. Consider the framework that I'll be outlining in this book to be your fast-pass. When you use what you learn here, you'll be able to move to the front of the line, which is reserved for effective leaders and happy employees.

I've put together this framework to help you improve your relationships with your boss, peers, and teammates. Through coaching and consulting with hundreds of clients over the years, I have developed and fine-tuned a model that consists of seven principles to help you hold difficult conversations.

My clients are probably much like you. They want to feel good about their work, and they want others to feel the same way. It's not an easy undertaking to achieve, but certainly doable. Here are the seven principles that will enable you to achieve similar results to some of my best clients.

The Seven Principles

Confidence

The first principle is confidence. It takes confidence to present your side of the conversation in a way that will have the other person engaged enough in the conversation to be open to hearing your thoughts on the matter at hand. I'll walk you through some exercises you can use to build confidence and share stories on how confidence helped others successfully conduct some pretty hair-raising conversations.

You'll learn ways to trust yourself, so you can confidently handle any challenging situation that may come your way. We'll explore the impact one-sided conversations have on business relationships and your career and what you can do as an employee to ensure your voice is heard. We'll also examine why you need to take the time to build a trusting relationship with someone, before jumping right in and saying what's on your mind, and what happens to those who don't.

Clarity

The second principle is clarity. If you've ever had a conversation with someone and left thinking, "What was their point?" then you know firsthand the importance of getting clear on what you hope to achieve *before* saying something. We'll also explore why it's important to listen with an open mind, so you can come to terms with an outcome that works for both parties.

Compassion

Next up is compassion. All too often, we approach conversations with little empathy. We don't take the time to understand what's really going on with the other person, whether an employee, a boss, or a coworker. We simply charge ahead and are then completely taken off guard when the conversation doesn't go as planned. We'll look at ways to gain a better understanding of where someone is coming from so that you can adjust your stand accordingly.

Curiosity

Principle four is curiosity. It's easy to jump to negative conclusions when someone says, "Can we talk?" Most people immediately get defensive when hearing these words. This chapter will explain how to use curiosity to move conversations from fear and apprehension to exploration, so both parties end up in a better place than where they started. I'll be providing you with prompts to help you launch the conversation on a positive note, as well as a list of open-ended questions to help you gain a better understanding of the situation at hand.

Compromise

Principle five is compromise. Let's face it. Most challenging conversations end in compromise, so why not start there? Think about all the time and energy you'll be saving when you enter the discussion with a plan in place that both parties can be moderately happy with. The focus here will be on asking for what you want and settling for getting most of what you asked for.

Credibility

Principle six is credibility. If you want people to listen to you, then you need to give them a good reason to do so. After all, your word is only as good as your actions. Saying things like, "You need to listen to me because I'm the boss" or "I know what I'm doing," when clearly you don't, can do more harm than good. Readers will learn how to take a step back and work on building credibility before powering forward.

Courage

We'll tie up the framework with principle seven, courage, and successfully navigating power dynamics in the workplace. Office politics is perhaps the most challenging situation employees face. This topic is not for the faint of heart, which is why I've saved this topic for the end. My hope is that having read this book, you'll have the skills and tools required to safely navigate through the political minefields that are part of every organization.

It takes courage to go into the "lion's den," and have a discussion with someone who perhaps sees things very differently than you or holds more power than you do in the organization. In this chapter, we'll look at some of the biggest obstacles that get in the way of having a productive conversation and what you can do to overcome these. I'll be sharing how others overcame some pretty challenging scenarios and how you can do the same.

As you move through this book, I encourage you to take the time to work through the exercises and incorporate what you're learning into your everyday conversations. Naturally, you may want to modify some of the scripts offered here to best match your personal communication style.

Give yourself permission to take some risks and try a few of the different approaches that you might have easily dismissed in the past. Who knows, you may decide that you (and your team members or your boss) like the newer version of yourself more than the person you were before reading this book.

Let's get the conversation rolling.

We're Heading for a Crash

Have you ever witnessed an accident about to happen while sitting there, unable to do anything about it? I have. In fact, it was my car that was hit.

Years ago, when I lived in Houston, Texas, I was waiting at a traffic light behind another car when I saw a vehicle coming toward me. I looked around to see if I could get out of the way, but there was nowhere for me to go. I braced myself as the driver of the car sideswiped my vehicle. I was lucky. I wasn't hurt, and some witnesses corroborated my story. It turns out the driver of the other vehicle was driving under the influence. I later learned this wasn't her first time doing so. One would hope that after her first DUI, her behavior would have changed. Unfortunately, this was not the case.

Sometimes it takes a while for people to get to a place where they understand their approach is harmful to others and may eventually end in their own demise. Let's hope this driver got the help she needed before doing any more harm.

It's been my experience that most people don't wake up in the morning thinking, "How can I make someone's day crappy?" Nor do they approach conversations with the goal of making someone weep. Yet, this sort of thing happens on a daily basis. And then, of course, there are the unsaid conversations. You know the ones that I'm talking about, as some of you probably have some of these conversations swirling around in your head. They go like this: "I'm so frustrated with Bill's work performance. I'm not going to assign him any more plum projects." Or, "If Donna makes one more wrong move, she's out of here!"

The thing about unsaid conversations is that they can create havoc without the other person even knowing there's a storm brewing. To me, unsaid conversations are the most dangerous. They remind me of the very small no-see-um insects. Pain can be inflicted by these insects before you are even aware of their existence, which means as the receiver (or the intended receiver), there's nothing you can do to protect yourself.

The Avoidance Epidemic: Why This Needs to Change—Stat!

The avoidance of difficult conversations has grown into a full-blown epidemic. In terms of personal communication, people are getting super good at avoiding sticky conversations, especially those related to politics. This is probably a good thing, given that no one ever comes out a winner in these sorts of conversations.

Most of us know at least one person (or we may be that person) who was fired and said, "I had no idea this was coming." Their response to being fired isn't about going on the defense, as a result of being let go. It's simply their truth.

There are enough stories of folks being fired with little to no warning, no feedback, and no help or support from their bosses to improve what was lacking to fill at least one mystery book—perhaps even a trilogy. That's the real crime here.

According to workplace resource startup Bravely, a whopping 70 percent of employees are avoiding awkward conversations with their boss, colleagues, and direct reports.[1] The fact that so many people are avoiding conversations is having a dramatic impact on the health and well-being of organizations and their employees. Here's how:

- New research from Joseph Grenny and David Maxfield, authors of *Crucial Conversations*, conducted in December of 2016 found that *every single* conversation failure costs an organization $7,500 and more than seven workdays.[2]

- An August 15, 2017, study, released by leadership development and conversation experts at Fierce, Inc. found that 53 percent of employees are handling "toxic" situations by *ignoring* them. By doing so, they are allowing toxic employees to continue to wreak havoc on the workplace.[3]

- A July 2008 report published by CCP Human Capital, found that employees spend 2.8 hours per week dealing with difficult situations—amounting to approximately $359 billion in paid hours.[4]

As a result, employee engagement and organizational trust are declining, while workplace stress is rising. We have to take action and slow this epidemic down, or we may never recover from the damage that is being done.

We have to start somewhere. Let's start with one conversation at a time.

The Conversation Equation

I've been a party to a number of workplace conversations, and here's what I've observed: It takes two people to have a conversation, although you wouldn't know it when hearing how most challenging workplace conversations go.

Here's what a typical workplace conversation sounds like:

Boss: Can we talk?

Employee: Okay.

Boss: You're not meeting my expectations.

Employee (looking bewildered): Uh, Okay.

Boss: I'm putting you on a performance improvement plan. You've got ninety days to turn things around.

Employee: Okay.

The boss leaves the conversation, thinking, "Hey, that went pretty well!" The employee leaves thinking, "What the heck was that all about?" (Okay, more than likely, the employee is thinking something else, which I can't very well include here.)

This could have been a very productive conversation and an opportunity for both parties to hit the reset button. In this case, the boss should use a technique I call the "success shuffle." The success shuffle is similar to the game of shuffleboard; only instead of taking turns moving a disk, each participant receives a turn moving the conversation forward.

The leader needs to take the initiative. "Can we talk?" followed by "You're not meeting my expectations" is like sending the first two disks flying off the board.

You need to start with a precision shot. For example, starting by highlighting something positive the employee has done recently is a better way to start the conversation off right. The rules of shuffleboard and the success shuffle are similar. Players alternately take turns, which is a good reminder for those who tend to dominate conversations. In the success shuffle, you don't get to speak until the other person responds, even if that means you sit in silence.

At first, this may feel awkward. You may be tempted to jump in and rescue the other person from the silence. Don't do it! Remember, this conversation may have been going on in your head for weeks, while in all likelihood, this is the first time the other person has heard what you're saying. Give the person you're speaking with time to process what's been said and to respond. Resist the temptation to formulate your next move until you see where the shot has landed.

Here's where the similarities to the game of shuffleboard and this process end. In the game of shuffleboard, players sling shots in an effort to knock opponents off their game. In life, this kind of behavior is known as one-upmanship. For one person to win, the other person has to lose. This is not at all what we're going for here. What we need here is a win-win.

Both the game of shuffleboard, as well as the success shuffle game of language can be improved significantly with patience and practice, which is why I suggest you immediately put to use the skills you're learning here. I've had many complicated work conversations over the years. I can say with 100 percent certainty that once you master the skills needed to conduct effective conversations, your life will change in ways you cannot even imagine.

Five Signs a Tough Conversation May Be Coming Your Way

People say all the time, "I would never have imagined…" or "I never saw this coming." Yet, in hindsight, the signs were all there. They just didn't want to see them.

I can relate. I mentioned earlier that I thought my relationship with my boss had gotten better. I wanted to believe this was the case *so* much that I ignored some of the telltale signs that would have indicated we were about to have one of *those* kinds of conversations. Had I been more aware, I could have been prepared, and the outcome may have been different. Or, at a minimum, the scarring I experienced from that day may never have occurred.

Sign Number One: You've Gone from Right-Hand Man to No Man's Land

You used to be your boss's right-hand person—the first one she turned to for help. She'd say things like, "I don't know what I'd do without you" or "Why can't everyone on the team have your work ethic?" Now, you're invisible. Your offers to help go in one ear and out the other. Nowadays, you wonder if she'd even notice if you stopped coming in for work.

A similar occurrence happened to a client of mine. "In the past, one of the biggest signs I missed that a tough conversation was coming was not noticing how irritated my boss was after I contradicted her in a customer service meeting. After that meeting, everything seemed to be normal except she hardly asked for my opinion anymore regarding strategic decisions, amongst other things. A few months later, she asked me if we could talk, left me waiting in her office for over ten minutes, and told me I was fired because I was too argumentative. I was absolutely blown away!"

Sign Number Two: Twitter-sized Conversations with Your Manager Are the New Norm

In the past, conversations with your boss often carried on for hours. The two of you would go back and forth with one another, brainstorming the next great idea. Now, you're lucky to get an email response back that is more than 280 characters when asking a question.

Sign Number Three: Your Boss Avoids You at All Costs

This one may seem like a no brainer, yet most people haven't a clue that *they're* actually the reason the boss is avoiding them. Instead, they convince themselves that their manager is overwhelmed and doesn't have time to exchange pleasantries. Or that their boss is not one of those touchy feely kinds of leaders you read about in articles on great leadership.

Before you dismiss your boss's behavior as being their problem and not yours, consider the following:

- Can you pinpoint a specific moment in time when your boss went from being friendly to being standoffish? Perhaps you failed to deliver your best work on a high-profile project. Or a family matter prevented you from keeping a commitment you made to your boss.

- Did you receive a rating on your latest performance review that was lower than expected with little explanation as to why this was so? You chose not to probe further, for fear your boss might say something you were not ready to hear.

- Have you been complaining a lot more lately rather than being more helpful to your manager? You didn't mean for this to happen. However, it appears you've made a common error of mistaking your boss for a friend.

Sign Number Four: You Can Do No Right

Your work is being sent back to you with loads of corrections and with little explanation. You do what most employees do. You accept the revisions and avoid asking how you might have gone off track. This pattern continues until the boss reaches a point where they no longer trust you to do the work you've been assigned.

You quickly conclude that your boss is nit-picky. You're frustrated, but most likely not as frustrated as your boss. Your boss asks to schedule a meeting with you. You put the date on your calendar, with little thought as to why you've been summoned to the boss's office.

Sign Number Five: Your Boss No Longer Returns Your Calls, Texts, or Emails

You've tried reaching out several times to speak to your boss about an important matter. Your calls go to voicemail. You try following up with an email. Again, no response. As a last resort, you text. Still no reply. You ask your teammates if they've had a hard time reaching your boss. They find your question puzzling, as they've noticed no difference in response time from your leader.

Your boss may be formulating a plan to address a situation with you. He or she is not looking forward to the conversation, so they do what many people in this situation do. They avoid *any* communication until they've mustered up the courage to say what's on their mind.

Don't make the fatal mistake most people make. No news (or, in this case, no response) is *not* good news. As soon as you realize you're being ghosted, make a plan to be seen by your manager. Do this even if you suspect this may be your last meeting with this person. It's better to know exactly where you stand than it is to remain in a state of flux.

Keep in mind that it's not uncommon for managers who are dissatisfied with staff members to avoid directly addressing issues that are bothering them. They will often dodge, deflect, procrastinate, and pray the whole problem will go away. Remember this the next time you sense a change in the way your boss is communicating with you.

Rather than sticking your head in the sand (right beside your boss), it's best to take steps to fix things *before* the situation gets to the point where your relationship is beyond repair. We'll go into detail on exactly how to do this throughout this book.

Creating the Right Conditions: Set the Stage for Successful Conversations

Preparation: Ready, Set, Go

The focus when planning for a difficult conversation should be on how to *create* something from this talk. Think about how to build an outcome that not only gets you through this situation, but also has you looking forward to the follow-up conversation that will bring you one step closer to what you're trying to achieve. With this in mind, think about where it's best to hold this exchange and when to address certain situations.

Location, Location, Location

Where you discuss a highly charged matter could very well determine how the other person reacts, and could directly impact the outcome you hope to achieve.

I was a newly hired department head who was involved in what began as a casual discussion with a subordinate hired by my predecessor. This employee told me they thought they had been hired to replace the former leader and wanted to know about some of the promises verbally made regarding the future. Specifically, pay, incentives, and future job movement were on hand.

At first, I was taken aback by the boldness and directness of the conversation. I asked questions to understand better how this employee perceived the future unfolding. The employee stated that the department's former head informed them that they would take over the department when he retired and would be entitled to executive benefits for longevity and compensation as an executive, which went with the new title. I asked for more detail into the executive benefit and salary piece they were alluding to, and the employee said that they would think that it would be similar to what I had received.

Because of this being an HR department and the nature of the jobs, we both had access to personal and confidential information, so I assumed that they knew the terms of my compensation package. I made the mistake of offering up not the specific amounts of my package but the general details of what was offered to me to stay as an executive of the company until retirement. Upon revealing this general information, the employee asked for a written document stating they would receive those same terms in the future. I declined and went so far as to say that they would not be getting the job because I now had the job, and I wasn't planning on leaving the position, nor would I be anointing a predecessor this early in my tenure. I asked that the employee drop the conversation as I realized I had said too much, and they had gotten so little in the way of answers. This left both the employee and myself in a tumultuous situation for future work engagement.

Looking back on the conversation and then moving forward, I knew I should not have entered into the conversation as casually as it started. I should have shut down the conversation and allowed for a more structured dialogue in a more professional environment than walking outside to the vehicles after the end of a long workday.

By doing so, I would have had time to investigate what may or may not have been said to this employee, prepared a more thoughtful response, and kept the focus on the employee—which is where it belonged.

A. J. Jenness SHRM-CP
VP/Director of HR, Admiral/Fremont Beverage

Like A. J., I learned firsthand how location can directly impact the outcome of a conversation. Early in my career, one of my managers decided to address a situation that was weighing heavily on his mind. He did so in the office elevator, which was fine when we were the only people riding up to our floor. However, what began as a productive conversation quickly fell apart as the elevator kept stopping and others got on.

There is a reason that hospital elevators have signs reminding staff not to discuss patient information in the elevator. Some conversations are not meant to be heard by others. You can't help but listen in on a juicy conversation when it's happening less than a few feet behind you. This is why *where* you hold a difficult conversation is as important as what you plan on saying. Yet, few people give enough thought to this.

Today's unique office environments can add a level of complexity in terms of where to best hold a challenging work conversation. Some people work in workplaces without walls, and a large number of employees are working virtually.

If your workspace doesn't afford you much in terms of privacy, try reserving a conference room with blinds for your meeting. When broaching topics, such as an employee termination or the need to place a team member on a performance improvement plan, consider whether it's best to have this conversation face-to-face with team members who work remotely.

Preparing for the Worst and Expecting the Best

I generally consider myself to be a somewhat optimistic person. However, when it comes to challenging work conversations, I've found that it's best to prepare for the worst. This way, no harm is done when things go better than planned.

Consider the following:

- **All possible outcomes when you ask, "Can we talk?"** There are only a limited number of responses that can occur when you pose this question. They are:

- "Sure!" followed by "I'm so glad you brought this up." In this scenario, you've just been given the green light. Keep your foot on the accelerator and steer the conversation as planned.

- Tears, followed by "Why do I have a feeling something bad is going to happen?" Here's where you're going to need to pump the brakes, to slow things down. Diving into a conversation with someone who is completely caught off guard (whether they should be or not is irrelevant here) will not get you any closer to where you want to be. In this situation, it's best to pause and allow the other person to regain their composure. Then assess whether it makes sense to continue the conversation or establish a time to reconvene.

- "No, this isn't a good time." You've just been asked to come to a complete stop. You're best response is something like, "Okay. Let's take out our calendars and establish a date and time for us to speak."

- "No." You've just hit a brick wall. It's hard to argue with a boss who says this or a coworker who doesn't want to engage. You'll have to decide how far you're willing to go to address this issue or if you're best off letting things be. If one of your direct reports says this to you, then of course you can't simply accept no for an answer. In this situation, you'll need to turn your question into a statement and say, "Perhaps you've misunderstood. We need to talk."

- **Staying cool as the conversation heats up.** If you're going to get to the heart of the matter, then tempers may flare. It's during times like these where you'll be tested to stay calm. Some people find it helpful to count to ten before responding. This allows them to catch their breath and gives them a few seconds to phrase their response in a way that won't add more fuel to the fire. Others find active listening works well to diffuse the situation. Reframing what someone else has said, and repeating this back to them, signals to the other person they've been heard. They are then usually more open to what's said next.

- **Focus on what you hear, rather than on how you want to respond.** Often, we're so busy thinking about how we will respond that we fail to deeply listen to what the person in front of us is saying. To help you avoid this misstep, consider asking clarifying questions, such as, "Can you say more about that?" or "Why do you feel this way?" This will help you stay engaged in the conversation. Challenge yourself to talk less during a difficult conversation and listen more. You'll be amazed at how much better conversations go when people feel they've been heard.

- **Avoiding the stuck ketchup syndrome.** Some of you may be old enough to remember the ketchup commercial where singer-songwriter Carly Simon sang the song "Anticipation" as we waited for the ketchup to pour out of the container slowly. I don't know about you, but I was pretty convinced that the ketchup was stuck and would never flow smoothly. Much to my surprise, once the ketchup started flowing, it didn't stop. Sometimes we have a hard time getting the juices flowing when discussing an uncomfortable situation. Yet, if we make an attempt to start, the conversation will begin to flow. Here's the thing about conversations: Both parties usually go back and forth more than once, which allows us plenty of opportunities to recraft our message, depending on how the other person responds. The key here is to be patient and give yourself permission to have a slow start. Your success in handling these situations won't be measured on how quickly you plow through them, but instead, on the taste you leave in people's mouths.

Anticipating Success

Have you ever argued with someone where you continued to push your agenda, even after you won? I have and know of many others who have done this as well. We're so focused on stating our position and proving that we're right that we completely miss the part where the other person says, "Okay, I can see where you're coming from. Where do we go from here?" Instead, we refer to our speaking points to ensure *everything* we've written down gets said.

Earlier I stated that it's best to go into these types of conversations expecting the worst. However, that doesn't mean you shouldn't be prepared for success. With enough practice and coaching, you'll learn how to effortlessly address these situations as part of everyday conversations with the people you work with. You'll also learn to pick up on the cues that indicate someone has gotten what you said and is ready to move forward with you.

In the next chapter, we'll explore the first principle for navigating difficult conversations at work, which is confidence. In my consulting and coaching practice, I have found that confidence is one area where small improvements can make a big difference in the way we present ourselves and how others see us, which is why I'm starting the conversation here.

KEY LEARNING POINTS

- Sometimes it takes a while for people to get to a place where they understand their approach is harmful to others and may eventually end in their own demise.

- Most people don't wake up in the morning thinking, "How can I make someone's day crappy?" Think about this before passing judgment and taking action that you may very well regret.

- The problem with unsaid conversations is that they can create havoc without the other person even knowing there's a storm brewing. What's left unsaid can do more damage than words that may be spoken.

- Avoidance of difficult conversations has grown into a full-blown epidemic. When deciding whether to begin a challenging discussion, consider whether you want to join the outbreak or be part of the cure.

- It takes two people to have a conversation, although you wouldn't know it when hearing how most challenging workplace conversations go. When having a conversation with someone, make sure you're not the only one doing all the talking.

- As tempting as it might be to stick your head in the sand to avoid a conversation that may be coming your way, it's best to take steps to fix things *before* the situation gets to the point where your relationship is beyond repair.

- Preparation matters—a lot! When preparing for a deep conversation with someone, remember to give considerable thought as to where you'll be holding this meeting, as well as the timing, as both factors can significantly influence what transpires after you are both done having your say.

- Prepare for the worst and expect the best. Think about *all* possible outcomes (both good and bad) that may occur when you say the words, "Can we talk?" Have a response ready to go to ensure the conversation remains on track.

- Don't forget to prepare for success. Be prepared for this moment so that you don't wind up saying more than needs to be said.

Endnotes

1 Understanding the conversation gap: Why employees aren't talking, and what we can do about it, Bravely, July 2019, https://learn.workbravely.com/hubfs/Understanding-the-Conversation-Gap.pdf?t=1533596048056&utm_campaign=smart%20brief%20test&utm_source=hs_automation&utm_medium=email&utm_content=64321921&_hsenc=p2ANqtz-_4k_KzRnQlCrerxB5Gr0XEMMWshlLmigMT3ElhTx6htsOUK3kcp7H-J_GAqZMvIAdILhbkkDX2sEDVSXIQdx9e-xqh8A&_hsmi=64321921 (archived at https://perma.cc/CCV6-MUW6)
2 Costly conversations: Why the way employees communicate will make or break your bottom line, VitalSmarts, 6 December 2016, www.vitalsmarts.com/press/2016/12/costly-conversations-why-the-way-employees-communicate-will-make-or-break-your-bottom-line/ (archived at https://perma.cc/4YFE-8DTH)
3 Toxic Employee Survey: 2017, Fierce, Inc., 15 August 2017, fierceinc.com/toxic-employees-survey-2017/ (archived at https://perma.cc/UJZ5-NEUJ)
4 Human capital report: Workplace conflict and how business can harness it to thrive, CCP, July 2008, img.en25.com/Web/CPP/Conflict_report.pdf (archived at https://perma.cc/9MTX-KAKK)

01

Confidence

Trusting Yourself and the Other Party

A difficult conversation tends to go best when you approach the conversation feeling self-assured, which is why I've chosen confidence as the first principle of *Can We Talk?*. Throughout this chapter, we'll be examining the connection between self-confidence and the need to trust yourself and others. I'll be sharing signs that indicate you don't trust yourself and will be offering up suggestions on what you can do about this. Included will be a discussion on mindset and the impact your beliefs have on your actions. I hope that your confidence in your ability to handle tough work conversations will rise as you challenge yourself to step forward and take on those conversations that you know need to happen.

Fear and self-confidence are inextricably linked, especially when it comes to having challenging conversations. Many of us are fearful that we're going to screw up a conversation and perhaps make things worse than they already are. Our fears are often unfounded and are reinforced by that little voice we hear in our head or that little guy or gal on our shoulder telling us untruths like, "This isn't going to go well" or "What makes you think you're the expert?" or "This person is never going to change." Simply put, you don't trust yourself, or you don't trust the person you're speaking with, which is why so many important conversations never take place. You figure, "Why bother?" So, you don't, which can lead to a host of other issues.

The "little voice" you're hearing is there to protect you, even when you don't need protection, and is caused by self-doubt. For example, you want to ask your boss for a well-deserved promotion. Yet, there's this voice in your head saying things like, "Are you kidding me? You're good, but you're not that great." Or, "Don't you think if you were ready for a promotion your boss would have given you one already?" This voice wants to protect you from the damage that might occur to your self-esteem should you not be awarded the job. Therefore, you don't ask for a promotion. You quickly regret your decision when your peer advances, especially if this person is now your new boss.

These voices are like little signs that point to one road and one road only—the road of self-doubt. Simply put, you don't trust yourself, *or* you don't have a trusting relationship with the person you're about to speak with. The goal here is to eliminate (or at least significantly reduce) self-doubt. You can increase self-confidence and trust. But to do so, you have to change your mindset and be open to taking a different path. You also have to be willing to take risks. We'll be setting a new course with our final destination being a street called trust throughout this chapter.

The Land of Should Have, Could Have, Would Have

In my work as an executive coach, clients often walk me through several different versions of the same conversation they've had with an employee, their boss, or a board member. First, they tell me what transpired, followed by the discussion that went on in their head. Often there is another version that many feel compelled to explain, which is what they *wished* they had said, and I hear many variations of: *should have, could have, or would have.* All of this second-guessing leads to exhaustion, followed by frustration, and often regret. Sound familiar?

Here's a conversation that recently took place between my coaching client, whom we'll call Don, and his boss Catherine. "My boss Catherine called me into her office the other day and raked me over the coals," Don said. This is a case where Don's second-guessing himself resulted in a difficult conversation going from bad to worse. I'll also show you how this situation could have been avoided.

Catherine: I expected this report to be on my desk when I arrived on Friday morning. I had no choice but to go into the executive leadership meeting without our findings. I was embarrassed when the CEO called upon me with a question about data included in our report, and I had nothing to share with him.

Don: We never received the revenue numbers from you. Therefore, we couldn't finish the report. You also handed us another assignment earlier in the week and instructed us to get that done. You know we're understaffed and can't hire anyone until you approve the requisition that's sitting on your desk.

After some reflection, Don concluded that he had handled the situation with his boss poorly. Don went on to tell me exactly what he should have said in his boss's office:

Don: I can certainly see why being called upon by the CEO and not having the information you needed in front of you to respond would have been embarrassing. I sincerely apologize for that. I take full responsibility for not coming to you on Wednesday when I first realized that we were still waiting on the revenue information needed to complete our report. I've learned a valuable lesson and can assure you it won't happen again.

The language that Don used with his boss made a bad situation worse. His manager wasn't looking for excuses. She was looking for an apology and assurances that she wouldn't find herself in this predicament again.

In Don's do-over conversation, he took complete responsibility for failing to deliver as promised. He apologized to Catherine for making her look bad in front of the executive team and vowed to do better. From my perspective, Don hit the bulls-eye when he shared with me what he should have said. He was right on target, knew what to say, yet, he didn't say it. Why? Because he didn't trust himself enough to do what he needed to do. Instead, he let the little guy on his shoulder cloud his judgment. That guy was saying, "Protect yourself at all costs. Don't be the fall guy." As a result, Don focused on placing the blame elsewhere, which didn't serve him well. Instead, he should have been looking for a way to reestablish trust with his boss. It bears mentioning that it took a long time for Don to recover from this mistake.

New Math: Why Things Aren't Adding Up

Admittingly, it's been a while since I attended school. However, I remember the concept of "new math," which is basically a more innovative way to approach a problem that results in the same answer you would have gotten had you used "old math." No matter which style of math you prefer, the equation 1 + 1 always adds up to two— or does it?

As I mentioned before, sometimes workplace discussions between two people include three or four voices: the little guy or gal sitting on people's shoulders, whispering sweet little nothings into their ears like, "Oh, you don't really want to say that, do you?" Or "You're just a guy pretending to be a boss. Everyone knows you don't know how to manage." That's when 1 + 1 can equal 3 or sometimes 4.

Some people can quickly quiet the voices in their heads or the little people on their shoulders. Then there are the rest of us who have difficulty speaking our minds for fear of what others will think. Instead, we let these conversations play out in our minds in a continuous loop, which can severely impact our mental health. We have to stop these kinds of internal discussions before they destroy us.

The Problem with Having Conversations in Your Head

I don't know about you, but I can spend hours talking to myself. I can easily come up with a dozen reasons why I'm not going to confront someone, along with another dozen reasons why I should. If we're keeping score here, the side that calls for nonconfrontation usually wins.

Here's what I've found to be true of conversations in your head.

- These kinds of conversations are for the sender, not the receiver. Here's what I mean by this. I never think about how the other person might react to something that I say in my head. The focus is on *me* and what I want to sling at someone else. Of course, by the time I'm done conjuring up all sorts of ways to express my thoughts and feelings, I'm fired up on all cylinders. So much so, that sometimes I even forget what the specific topic was that I wanted to address! Which leads to my next observation.

- One-sided conversations with yourself go nowhere. How can you possibly resolve a misunderstanding or an issue you may be having with someone if they have no idea there's a problem? You can't!

We've all participated in the silence is golden game. Someone says, "Is there something on your mind that you'd like to talk about?" You say, "No." You're not ready to discuss the situation or you think they'll respond negatively to what you have to say. They probe a little bit more, and you react with abbreviated answers like, "Everything's fine" or "I don't want to talk about it." From that point forward, you do your best to avoid one another.

In reality, there is no way for you to know for sure how the other person will respond. It's like trying to play chess with one player. Your time would be better spent telling the person what's on your mind and hearing their reaction *before* preparing a response.

The simplest way to get things out of your head is to write them down. Take a moment and jot down what's on your mind. Is the matter worth further discussion? If the answer is yes, then schedule a time to speak with the other person. Some of you may be thinking, "I'm not having this conversation because I don't know what to say." That's not uncommon. Here's how to overcome this hurdle. To prepare for the meeting, write down some bullet points of what you'd like to get off your chest. You can take this one step further by scripting out the conversation ahead of time. Don't worry about committing your script to memory. It's better if you don't sound overly rehearsed. If you need to, you can always refer to your notes. However, as you work through this, if you begin to realize that something is merely an annoyance or a one-off situation, then consider letting it go.

Trust Me: Why You Need to Trust Yourself

Every now and again, I'll watch some home movies that show me brazenly prancing through my old neighborhood in Queens, New York, at the ripe old age of three. I was bold as well as confident. I trusted that I'd somehow make it back home safely. Of course, there was always a parent a few feet behind me. At the time, I probably didn't realize this, as I appeared to be a woman on a mission, without any regard as to who or what was around me.

I don't quite remember what age I was when I began to trust others more than I trusted myself. All I know is that at some point I began to seek approval from people whose opinions I thought mattered more than mine. It might have been in elementary school, where I was first taught that the teacher is always right. I know now that this is not true.

What about you? Do you trust others more than you trust yourself? If so, why is this so? I'm guessing that from time to time, people seek your advice. Why do they trust your opinion more than their own? Why would they ask for your point of view if they didn't value your take on a situation? Something to think about the next time you start to second-guess yourself.

For most of us, including myself, self-trust can be tricky. We tend to doubt ourselves, or perhaps we hang onto memories of a situation that didn't exactly go as planned. Or maybe our gut tells us to do one thing and our mind tells us to do another. These experiences make it difficult to trust yourself and create challenges with personal and work relationships. No one knows this more than one of my coaching clients. When you read her story, you'll understand a bit more why she spent a great deal of time second-guessing herself about a management decision she knew had to be made.

This is my client's story.

We were entering our busiest season, and my boss asked if I knew anyone looking for work. I immediately thought of my sister, who was available and had the skills needed to help us get through the rush.

Early on in her employment, my sister began making careless mistakes. As soon as this happened, I considered calling her into my office and asking her about this. However, I didn't. I kept second-guessing myself. Every time I told myself that this week would be the week I'd have this discussion, the little voice inside my head would tell me to wait. I would make up excuses like maybe I was expecting too much of a new employee, or perhaps I didn't train her properly. The mistakes continued until it got to the point where I could no longer look the other way.

I called my sister into my office and casually asked, "Hey, have you gotten back to these customers?" She hesitated and said, "I don't remember. I'll check." Then she wouldn't get back to me. She missed numerous deadlines and never gave me a heads-up. When I finally did confront her about this, she'd say things like, "I thought someone else was taking care of this," or "Don't worry, I'll get to it." This went on for several months.

I finally hit my breaking point when one of our dedicated long-term employees, who was picking up the slack for my sister, threatened to quit. It was at that point that I realized how much damage I had done by second-guessing myself and being afraid to confront this situation.

I scheduled a call over Zoom since, at the time, we were all working remotely due to the Covid-19 crisis and didn't tell her what the meeting was about, but I think she knew. I began our call by saying, "Your performance has been substandard and is impacting the rest of the team." I then went on to list specific performance issues and the impact this was having on the organization. She didn't contest anything that I stated. I then said, "I have no choice but to fire you." She said she understood.

It's been several months since that conversation, and I still think about it. I know in retrospect it was the right thing to do. In fact, if I had to do it over again, I think I still would have hired my sister, as she had the right skills and could start immediately. Most importantly, I should have trusted myself and my ability to manage this situation. I knew early on that things weren't going to work out. Yet, I allowed my sister to remain in her job way longer than I should have, which in the end wasn't fair to the people I managed or my sister.

Anonymous

When my client first shared some of her employees' challenges, I couldn't understand why she hesitated to terminate this employee. The pieces began to fall into place when she later revealed that the employee she was about to fire was *her sister*. While my client says if she had to do it over again, she'd still hire her sister, that's a move I'd try to avoid. It's challenging enough to manage people. Now imagine going home to your parents and having to explain to them that you just fired their daughter!

My client started to second-guess herself when she first realized her sister was making costly mistakes. She later confessed to me that she knew all along what needed to be done and that she didn't trust her ability to handle the situation the correct way. Had she trusted herself and addressed the situation as it unfolded, she would have avoided what she described to me as "one of the most stressful periods of my life."

When meeting with her sister, my client made some common mistakes. She took her sister's word at face value, even though the evidence she had didn't align with what her sister was saying. She also didn't come out and tell her sister what would happen next if her performance levels remained the same. Here's a better way to handle a sticky situation like this one.

The moment she realized that something was amiss, my client could have called her sister into her office and said the following: "I need your help. It appears that some customer concerns are still pending. Let's go line by line and see which customers are waiting for a return call." Starting the conversation by asking for help demonstrates to the other person that you're there to find a solution and not looking to merely place blame for the problem. At this point, her sister may have opened up and asked for additional support to complete her work. My client could have then discussed whether or not her sister enjoyed this job and if this work was a good match for her skill set.

Let's say her sister responded by saying that she loved her job and felt this was the perfect position for her. This is when I'd advise my client to go deep and not just skim the surface. Perhaps she could have said something like, "I can appreciate that. However, we have to discuss your overall job performance. Within the past few weeks, you've made three significant mistakes, which have resulted in severe customer service issues." I'd then advise my client to present her sister with concrete evidence that these customer service problems were directly related to her poor job performance. I'd take this conversation one step further and let her sister know that if certain performance expectations were not met, this could lead to further disciplinary action up to and including termination. By doing so, my client would have then laid out her expectations and had a roadmap to follow should her sister continue to underperform.

Having second thoughts about what to say, or whether or not you should even say something at all, is common when faced with a difficult conversation, especially when you lack confidence in your ability to strategize your next move. As you can see from the example above, taking time to develop a roadmap can be extremely helpful and will help keep you on course.

It's understandable to second-guess yourself on occasion, especially if you're faced with a situation you've never encountered. However, if second-guessing is your go-to move, then it's time for a course correction. To do this, you have to first acknowledge you have a problem before you can remedy the situation. Once you recognize that you have a habit of second-guessing yourself, your next move is to work on trusting yourself more.

Practices to Overcome Self-Doubt

Here are some things you can do to enhance your ability to trust yourself. Let's begin with starting your day off right.

START YOUR DAY WITH A POSITIVE MINDSET

No doubt you're familiar with the term "mindset over matter." I can attest from personal experience that this saying is more than just three words you put on one of those motivational posters that hang in the company lunchroom, which is why I find it extremely helpful to begin each day with an affirmation. Affirmations are positive, specific statements that help to overcome self-sabotaging negative thoughts. When you look in the mirror each morning, tell yourself something positive. To quote the wise words of Buddha: "What we think, we become."

Here are some of my favorite affirmations to help you positively start your day. Feel free to use these or come up with your own:

- I can do whatever I set my mind to.
- What other people think of me doesn't make me who I am.
- I'm good enough.
- I'm in charge of how I feel.
- Today is going to be a great day!
- My life matters.
- Life is great!
- I'm smart and capable.
- I have so much value to offer others.

Here are some of the many benefits you'll receive when you build your confidence.

BUILD BENCH STRENGTH

Rather than attempting the most difficult tasks or conversations at hand, start with the ones you believe you've got a pretty good chance of handling reasonably well. Let's say you have to provide feedback to two people on your team who are not performing up to standard. The first team member is trying very hard but is a bit disorganized. You're now at a point where you can no longer look the other way.

The other employee refuses to accept feedback and blames everyone else for his shortcomings. You know you have to address this situation. However, you hesitate because you're relatively sure how they will react when you take this on.

I've heard advice from others who say you should tackle the most challenging situations first. You know, get the bad stuff out of the way. That advice may work for people who are good at diffusing situations and are great at quickly getting to the heart of the matter. You may not be there yet, which is why I'm suggesting you get a few wins under your belt before going into the lion's den.

Speak with the disorganized employee first. Offer suggestions to help this employee better organize their work. After you've completed this task, schedule a date and time to speak with your other employee. You can push this date out a week or two to give you ample time to finish reading this book.

BE DECISIVE

I once worked with a leader who would make a decision and then change his mind. He drove me and everyone else around him crazy. Imagine how much time this leader wasted as a result of overthinking everything. Or maybe you don't have to imagine if this story sounds a lot like you.

Being decisive requires you to make choices and adjust along the way. Forget trying to be flawless. Effective decision-making is about considering your past experiences, analyzing the current situation, making a risk-reward comparison, and, most importantly, believing in yourself.

Here's an exercise you can use to help you become a more decisive person:

1 Write down a decision that you need to make.

2 Quickly jot down options worth consideration. (Note: do not go back to this list and add more options.)

3 Next to each option, record all the pluses and minuses associated with that choice.

4 Select the best alternative.

5 Now, move onto the next decision.

Developing confidence has greater benefits than enabling you to have more productive conversations. People who trust themselves implicitly make better decisions in choosing who to be around and how to show up every day. Generally speaking, they're happier and less stressed out than those who are always second-guessing themselves.

What have you got to lose? Pick a couple of ideas that feel right to you or push you a bit out of your comfort zone and give them a try.

INCREASE POSITIVE SELF-TALK

Look, we seem to have no problem with negative self-talk. How often do you tell yourself you're not good enough to do something? Does your mind immediately go to thoughts like, "I'm terrible at that," or "Why would anyone choose me for this job, promotion, or project?" or "How on earth could I ever have a conversation like that?"?

Now imagine what would happen if you took your negative self-talk and turned it into positive self-talk. What if instead of convincing yourself you were terrible at doing something, you told yourself that perhaps you're not the best. However, with practice, you could be decent and maybe even great at something. What if instead of asking yourself why anyone would choose you over someone else for a job, promotion, or project, you said to yourself, "These people would be lucky to have me on their team!"?

Now let's apply this idea to a conversation that you've been avoiding. Rather than thinking, "Oh, boy. There's no way this is going to go well," you say to yourself, "With preparation and practice on my part, we should be able to have a productive conversation that will enable us to move forward."

Here are a few more tips to help you build self-confidence.

MAKE NOTE OF YOUR SUCCESSES

At the end of each day, write down one or two successes you experienced that day. Keep this in a journal or pin this list up on your bulletin board. Don't waste time worrying about whether or not something is worthy of being considered a success. You're the judge *and* jury here.

Each morning, before you begin your workday, review your success list. This list is an excellent reminder of how capable you are and will help you start your day off positively.

BE KIND TO YOURSELF

Rarely will everything go according to plan, which is why you need to forget being perfect. Instead, when conversations don't go as well as you hoped they would, take time to analyze what, if anything, did go well. Ask yourself what you could have done differently to achieve a better result.

Consider seeking feedback from a trusted colleague or a coach or mentor. Sharing how a conversation went with someone you trust to tell you the truth will prevent you from overthinking things. Chances are, you did way better than you think!

Signs You Don't Trust Yourself (and What to Do about It)

Here are some signs that you don't trust yourself and what to do about it.

You Have a Hard Time Recognizing, Understanding, or Believing in Your Innate Value and Worth

Perhaps you were told, by someone you trusted, that you weren't smart or that you'd never amount to anything. Maybe this was said to you more than once by a parent or even your boss. You bought into whatever was stated about you and now you can't rid yourself of these feelings.

First off, consider the source. Was the person who told you these things knocking you down to make themselves feel or look better? Did others mentally abuse this individual? Did you seek their opinion or were they delivering unsolicited feedback? The last question is essential, as unsolicited advice is for the sender—not the receiver.

Now that some time has gone by, are you in agreement with their conclusion? If the answer is no, then throw the baggage that's weighing you down off the train. I'll explain exactly how to do this further on in this chapter. If you're unsure whether these people are right, or you still have a negative self-image, consider getting some professional help.

You Often Defer to Others

You know the answer to a question being asked in a meeting, yet you wait for others to speak before offering your response. You're worried about how you'll look if no one else agrees with what you have to say. That's the least of your problems. A number of my coaching clients defer to others in meetings and find this kind of behavior is limiting their career options. Remaining silent while other people steal your thunder does more harm than good.

The next time you're in a meeting and a topic comes up that's in your wheelhouse, ask yourself, "What's the worst that can happen if I speak up?" Then jump right in and contribute. After all, no one is shooting at you. What you have to say could very well be right on target or a springboard to another idea worth consideration.

You Believe What Others Say More Than You Believe in Yourself

You know something to be true. Yet, the moment someone challenges your assumption, you immediately cave.

You're in a particular role for a reason. Somewhere along the way, someone saw something in you that made them want to hire you. If you don't believe you're deserving of the job you're in, then why would anyone else believe this? The next time someone challenges you, whether this person is your coworker, superior, or employee, take a pause. Count to ten. Then ask yourself this one simple question: "What evidence do I have that this person is right and I am wrong?" If after asking this question, you believe there's a fairly good chance you're correct, then be prepared to state your case. Here are some conversation starters you can use to begin the discussion and build confidence:

- "I can appreciate why you might feel this way. Perhaps I haven't explained myself as clearly as I thought I had."
- "I understand what you're saying. However, have you considered…"
- "Help me to understand why you believe this is the best course of action."
- "I appreciate your point. With your permission, I'd like to continue to explore our options here."
- "Thank you. That's an interesting idea. However, the data supports my findings. Let's discuss this further."

- "You know I've always valued your opinion. However, I'd be remiss if I didn't push back here."

You Rarely Try New Things

When is the last time you said yes to something that was totally out of your comfort zone? If it's taking you longer than a minute or two to come up with something, then you've just run into another sign that you don't trust yourself as much as you should.

Some people think that sticking with the same routines is about knowing oneself well enough not to take excess risks; it's actually the opposite. Trusting yourself means that you're in a place where you're willing to step out of your comfort zone and do new things.

I remember the first (and last) time I parasailed. I was hanging out with some new friends I had made in Australia, who invited me to observe them parasailing. I enthusiastically said yes. I watched from the sidelines as they worked with the parasailing instructor, and then they took off, flying above the hill! I thought that looked like a really cool thing to do. After my friends were up in the air, the instructor turned to me and asked me if I wanted to give it a go. I thought about all the reasons why doing this was a terrible idea, and then said yes. I trusted myself enough to know that no matter how things went, I'd be okay.

I suppose you think this is going to be one of those stories where the hero (me) goes sailing off fearlessly into the sunset. Actually, the opposite happened. As soon as I went to take off, the winds began to pick up. I got caught in a crosswind and wound up tumbling down the hill. My body hurt a bit from the fall, but not as much as my ego. Other than that, I was okay and survived to face another day.

Experiences, like the one I just described, make us who we are. Your version of a bold move may be standing up to your boss and telling that person the way they're speaking to you is unacceptable. Or perhaps you had to fire an employee who was a friend. Things didn't go exactly as planned. However, this ex-employee still waves hello when you see one another at church.

We're better than we think we are, even if (or perhaps because) we've had a few mishaps along the way. Go ahead. Extend yourself beyond your comfort zone. Fear will fade as you begin to get some successes under your belt. Take the baggage you're carrying and set it down. Now, don't you feel lighter and a bit more nimble?

Using Confidence to Navigate Difficult Conversations

Remember the first time you went to the gym and lifted weights? I do. I thought I could handle a lot more weight than I could. Boy, did my body suffer the next day. However, I didn't let my discomfort or my ego deter me. I went back the next day, and the day after, and built up my strength.

There's no magic diet or pill for strengthening your inner trust muscle. That's probably a good thing, as false promises are just that. The way to build inner trust is to establish and commit to a routine. The keyword here is commit, as we all know people with gym memberships who rarely use them. Of course, these same people wonder why they're not making any progress in their health goals! Here's a real-life example of how one executive used confidence to successfully charge through an extremely tough conversation.

Confidence and Trust

As mentioned earlier, sometimes conversations stall or derail because we don't have a trusting relationship with the other party. Here's a case in point.

Working in law enforcement for over twenty-nine years, you learn many lessons. Midway in my career, recently promoted to a captain position as the first female in a predominantly male office, establishing trust was more than a priority. My approach coming into a new environment was to observe and handle immediate issues based on a risk assessment analysis along with urgency dictated by the profession in policing. With regard to personnel issues, I felt it would be a good strategy to take the time to become familiar with employees, look over past performance in their personnel files, and allow myself time to develop a rapport and then a relationship. That approach played out much better in my notes and thoughts than it did upon arriving at the office on my first day.

My second-in-command, a lieutenant, had been given the charge of overseeing operations before my assignment. As I quickly discovered, he carried the interim title loosely. Briefed and prepared, I knew ahead of time the office was behind in meeting significant timelines for reporting, absenteeism was high, there was lack of supervision on shift schedules, morale was acidic, and overtime was well outside of the budget. Still thinking I could employ some of those initial approaches, I had to make a hard pivot to moving from relationship building to being more authoritative after receiving pressure from those above me. It took me off guard, the swift expectancy of their demands; it was only the first day. However, I was also newly promoted and on probation. After a few pleasantries around the office to introduce myself and complete the "Golden Hour," I met with the lieutenant in my office.

He had no idea the train was traveling down the tracks and he was sitting on the rails. Not new to counseling, but new to commanding, I said to him, "Supervisors need to be working, not all on vacation at the same time. I need you to make sure they are monitoring overtime, hard to do if they're not here. At the same time, absenteeism is high because there's no one being held accountable. Much of this stems from lack of leadership and holding people to the fire, until now."

He sat back in his chair, looked at me wide-eyed, and said, "Excuse me, you have no idea what I've had to deal with while there has been no captain for months in this office. You come in here and tell me what's not right and then want me to snap to and get all these things done. I know there's a lot messed up right now, but you don't even know what's going on." After giving myself a moment of not flinching at his tone, but internally churning over my next move, it came to me. "I know it's not something I want to have to talk with you about on the first day either. And, you're right. It will take me a while to know the command and all that's going on. That's why I need you to work with me as we resolve these issues. This is what I need to get done, and it's our responsibility to work on them with urgency. Is this something you can do?" He was silent and then surrendered to the moment, agreeing to the work at hand.

I didn't have time to build a deeply connected trust relationship with my lieutenant, but I was able to plant seeds for a future harvest. My approach was shortsighted until I took the time to use active listening when he had the courage to share what he was feeling. It was a moment where I could have chosen to slay him or hear him—choosing enmity or empathy. And considering, is this the hill to falter on? Or do we move forward unified to stand in the larger battles, of which we had many? I've found the success of leadership is not built in a silo of ourselves; it's made through the collective rumbling and reckoning of many.

Jonni Redick
President, JL Consulting Solutions

Unfortunately, you don't always get to control the timing of when you have to have a tough work conversation. Had Jonni waited, she would have run the risk of losing the respect of other team members. The chaos the department was experiencing may have worsened and put the public at risk. She had to weigh out the risks of letting things ride, until such time as she had established trust, or immediately taking action.

Here's what Jonni did well. She was direct and open with her employee regarding the current status of the department. She told her employee what she needed and then asked him if he was up to the task. By doing so, she was able to quickly bring this employee over to her side, where together, they were able to resolve the issues that were weighing the department down.

If you find yourself in a similar situation, I'd suggest that you have the conversation as soon as you notice there's a problem. Most leaders will wait. They'll hope and pray that things get better. Rarely is this ever the case.

You owe it to your employees to provide them with honest feedback, which is what Jonni did. Perhaps without even knowing it, she started the process of building trust with her employee by being willing to take on this challenging situation early in their relationship.

Trust: The Cornerstone of All Relationships

Have you ever done something *willingly* for someone whom you didn't trust? The key word here is willingly. Sure, we've all done things because we had to. And when we do, we usually don't put our heart and soul into getting something done. We do the minimum. Now compare this to when someone whom you trust and respect asks you to do something. Chances are you do what they've asked you to do, and then some. Low levels of trust may help to explain why, when you're having a challenging conversation at work with an employee, peer, or boss, things don't go according to plan.

Bank of Trust

Many years ago, when our daughter Lexi was seven years old, my husband Ron took her to the bank to open up a savings account. Ron intended to use this visit to the bank as a learning opportunity to teach our daughter how to be fiscally responsible. He also wanted Lexi to understand the theory behind compound interest, so that she would get into the habit of saving at a young age. What happened instead is that we all learned a valuable lesson.

The bank manager was explaining what would transpire with my daughter's savings, including a discussion on interest and bank fees. At the time, interest rates on savings accounts were hovering around 6 percent, which sounds like a lot by today's standards. The manager went on to say they'd be taking out eight dollars a month as a service fee on her modest $300 savings account.

My husband told me that as the manager kept on talking, our daughter appeared perplexed. She later confided in him that she couldn't wrap her head around the idea that in the end, she would be paying the bank to hold her money, since the monthly fee far exceeded what she would be making in interest. She turned to her dad and said, "Why would I want to do this? I'm losing money here."

My husband was speechless. Lexi was right to ask this question. The bank manager failed to establish trust with our daughter. She didn't explain that once Lexi had a certain amount in her account, the fees would go away. Lexi did what any other smart investor would do. She picked up her piggy bank and left and deposited her money in a bank that offered no-fee accounts for young savers.

I use this bank of trust example all the time in my coaching. I explain to my clients the importance of making deposits into their bank of trust savings account, as well as how to do so, and what happens when you need to make a withdrawal and your account is empty. Here's what I tell them.

You never know when you're going to need to ask someone for something. If you've made some trust deposits into the account that you have with this person, then you stand a good chance of being able to make a withdrawal (asking for something and having them say yes) when you need it. If the account is empty... well, you can guess how the conversation will probably go.

Here are ten ways to establish a healthy trust account:

1 Be completely honest in your dealings with others.

2 Do something for someone else, before asking them to do something for you.

3 Do what you say you will do.

4 Step up and have someone else's back during a meeting.

5 Give praise in front of others.

6 If you fail to do something that was asked of you, let the person know *before* they find out from someone else.

7 Give credit where credit is due.

8 Admit when you are in the wrong.

9 Apologize for your mistakes.

10 Volunteer to help someone in need.

Now let's apply this concept to a common situation that happens at work. In the first scenario, the person making the request doesn't have enough in their account to make a withdrawal. The second example demonstrates what happens when you have saved and planned for a rainy day.

Setting the Scene

You've been on the job for less than a year, and you'd like to request time off during your company's busy season. You know you can get all of your work done before you go. However, your boss has no idea if this is so.

SCENARIO NUMBER ONE

Several months ago, one of your coworkers unexpectantly went out on medical leave, thereby leaving your boss scrambling to cover this position. You stepped up and volunteered to work late and on weekends to help your boss through this challenging period. You did so while keeping up with your work.

You've done a great job of establishing a trusting relationship with your manager. You say to your boss, "I know I haven't been here long enough to qualify for vacation time officially. I also know December happens to be the busiest time of the year for our department. However, would you consider granting me a few days off so I can visit my family over the holidays? I'm willing to come in the weekend prior, to make up the time, and promise my work will be complete before I depart."

You've got a trusting relationship with your boss and you've done a nice job of presenting your case for time off, which includes your plan for completing your work before leaving. Your request is approved.

SCENARIO NUMBER TWO

Your boss calls the team together and shares the news that your coworker is taking a medical leave. She then asks for volunteers to take on some of your colleague's tasks. You keep your head down and pretend to be taking copious notes.

In a meeting with your boss, she reveals that she's feeling extremely stressed about completing certain goals on time, now that your team is down a person. You respond by saying, "Yeah, I've got a ton on my plate and have no idea if I'll even be able to complete everything that's been assigned." Several weeks later, you approach your boss and say, "I know it's our busy season, but I sure could use some time off. I'd like to take vacation time next Tuesday and Wednesday. Can you approve this for me? I'll do what I can to get through my to-do-list."

Your request is denied. It should come as no surprise that your request has been declined. You haven't made any deposits into your trust account with your boss. She has no reason to believe you will be able to get everything done prior to leaving. In fact, she's fairly sure you won't, given that you told her you don't think you have the bandwidth to complete what's already been assigned. You also failed to give before asking for something. The lesson here is that you can't make a withdrawal when there is nothing in your account. This rule applies in banking, as well as in business.

In the next chapter, we'll be discussing the second principle, which is clarity, and the need to get clear on exactly what you wish to get out of a conversation, before charging forward.

KEY LEARNING POINTS

- Lots of people are having "should have," "could have," "would have" conversations inside their heads. All of this second-guessing leads to exhaustion, followed by frustration, and often regret.

- One-sided conversations with yourself are time wasters. These conversations go nowhere. You can't possibly know what the other person might say until you speak with them.

- Consider writing down what you want to say to someone. Then, ask yourself if the matter is worth further discussion. If the answer is yes, then schedule a time to speak with the other person.

- If something is merely an annoyance or a one-off situation, then consider letting it go.

- You can't expect others to trust you if you don't trust yourself.

- To enhance your ability to trust yourself, use positive self-talk, note your successes, and be kind to yourself.

- Signs that you don't trust yourself include not believing in your innate value and worth, often deferring to others, and rarely trying new things. The way to overcome this is to develop your inner trust muscle.

- Take note of your successes. You're much better than you think.

- To strengthen your inner trust muscle, start each day with a positive affirmation. Build bench strength by starting with tasks and conversations you're reasonably sure you'll succeed with and work your way up to the more challenging situations.

- Making a withdrawal from your trust account when you don't have enough "funds" in it will result in relationship bankruptcy, which you may never fully recover from.

02

Clarity

Making Your Point Clearly and
Listening with an Open Mind

You'll never get where you're going if you don't know where you want to go, which is why, when dealing with difficult situations, you must have clarity on where you want to go before heading out to have a conversation. This is why I've chosen clarity as one of the seven principles for navigating difficult conversations at work. With this in mind, you have to establish the right objective and give consideration to a number of factors that will help you prepare for a high-stakes conversation. It's also important to plan for the worst and expect the best, which I'll explain in more detail in this chapter. We'll also be discussing the need to assess your readiness to proceed as well as how to handle difficult conversations remotely. Advice on how to keep your cool when things heat up and speaking in a way that will allow others to hear you loud and clear will be explored more fully. Finally, we'll end this chapter with a discussion on why the need to be right can bring about the wrong results and what you can do to avoid this.

Let's Be Clear Here

How often have you walked away, after chatting with someone, with a confused look on your face? The meetings may have lasted thirty minutes, or even longer, yet you still had no idea what transpired.

Perhaps it was one of those meetings where your boss placed you on a performance improvement plan. Your manager was speaking so fast that your mind couldn't catch up. Or maybe your coworker was asking you to provide them with some assistance. They were a bit unsure what they specifically needed from you. All they knew is that they could have used your help. You may have said no to their request because you were uncertain about how much time would be needed from you to assist them. Or worse, you may have said yes just to stop this perplexing exchange, even though you weren't fully committed. You then let your coworker down because you didn't have the skills or bandwidth to help.

Most meetings ramble because people wait until the last minute to figure out precisely what they want to happen *before* beginning the meeting. Some people never figure this out before starting, which explains why we often leave these kinds of discussions shaking our heads in confusion. That was me over twenty-five years ago. I was the person who, after speaking with my boss, walked out of the meeting shaking my head in confusion. Here's what transpired.

One of the co-owners of the company came to me and out of the blue ranted off a list of things he was not happy with. He dashed out of my office as quickly as he had arrived, without so much as giving me a chance to ask any questions. My first thought was, "Where the heck is this coming from?" followed by "What an ___" (you fill in the blank). I went home that night and replayed the conversation over and over again. Needless to say, I didn't get much sleep.

The next morning, the co-owner walked into my office and asked me if I had a second. I said, "Sure." And then he did something that surprised me even more than the "little chat" we had had the day prior. He apologized. He said he had gone home and told his wife what he had said to me. She told him he was an ___ (yep, the exact word that I was thinking). I told him his wife was right. Hey, she was!

He then went on to say that he hadn't thought through exactly what he wanted to say and how I might react. Nor was he clear in his own head where he wanted us to go from here. His apology arrived a day late. The night prior, I made the decision to check out of the organization. When I left, I didn't leave the company. I left him.

It's been over twenty-five years since that memorable encounter, and I still can't get this conversation out of my head. People share similar stories with me all the time, which indicates to me that we still have a lot of work to do in terms of clarity and workplace conversations. Here's a true story, shared by one of my clients, about what can happen when you don't have clarity.

A senior leader for our organization was hired two years ago. In the first few months, he exhibited enthusiasm, was knowledgeable about topics, and presented multiple ideas. In meetings, he was given assignments, his input was solicited, and the expectation was he would follow up, but he did not. The behavior of not seeing things through continued. This shortfall also affected his peers, who expected his follow-through and needed his participation.

The behavior of not seeing things through continued even after this initial period.

A one-on-one conversation ensued that addressed his presence and commitment to the organization. I met with the employee in my office; I stated, "There seems to be a clear disconnect between how you view yourself and your accomplishments and what your colleagues are saying." He stated, "I don't understand and would like specifics." I stated examples, "Emails stating solutions with no follow-up or collaboration, lack of follow-up on key projects, leaving early, and absence of visibility." I asked him if he was committed to the role. He stated he was but was not aware of the image he was portraying. We decided to work on the weaknesses, and if not resolved over the course of four months, we would have further discussion about his future in the organization.

In my opinion, in the initial one-on-one discussion, the expectation was to deliver on the assignments. However, the employee did not see this, nor was it made clear. In hindsight, the conversation was about his commitment to the organization and presence. It should have connected his lack of follow-up and attention directly to being a team player and his direct responsibilities to the team. A more direct conversation may have avoided this now more difficult situation. Things have since deteriorated further, to the point colleagues and superiors have noticed.

Ronald Bryant
President, Western and Northern Regions
Baystate Health

As you can see from Ron's story, clarity is critical for resolving a difficult situation. Otherwise, you may wind up like Ron and find yourself going down a path to nowhere. Ron's first clue that the message he intended to deliver was getting lost in translation was when his employee said he was not aware of the image he was portraying. Ron wasn't talking about image—he was talking about poor work performance. Had he picked up on this, he could have redirected the conversation back to the performance issues impacting the team, which is the behavior that Ron wanted to see change. Ron also spent considerable time discussing this employee's commitment to the organization, rather than the underlying issue—lack of follow-through. In being more direct, he could have said something like, "I'm talking with you because your lack of follow-up and attention is posing problems and affecting other members of the team."

It's interesting to note that Ron thought he was making his point clear. However, in retrospect, he realized this was not the case. To ensure his message was hitting the mark, Ron could have asked some clarifying questions after presenting his case, questions like, "What's your understanding of what I just said?" or "What exactly are you committing to do differently as a result of our conversation?" If the employee response was in any way off base, Ron would have then had the opportunity to say, "Hold on. I think you're missing my point. Let me be specific here." He could have then spelled out exactly how he saw the situation and his expectations going forward.

Getting clear and expressing precisely what you mean has to be a priority if we are to stand a chance of stopping the mass exodus of employees fleeing organizations in search of better bosses. We'd also be able to dramatically reduce the cost of employee turnover if we were more clear in our conversations.

Establishing the *Right* Objective

Too often, the main objective for people who are about to enter a tricky conversation is to get it over as quickly as possible. If that's your objective, don't be surprised if things don't go according to plan.

Keep in mind that you may have had plenty of time to think about what you want to say. However, the person you're speaking to is often hearing this for the first time.

The success of any challenging conversation will be decided long before the conversation starts, which is why you need to first come to terms with what you want for the relationship. Do you see a particular conversation as an opportunity to clear the air and move forward? Or is this meeting merely a formality—meaning HR says you have to have a certain number of discussions on a particular topic before terminating an employee?

You may be wondering why knowing this is so important. How much time you devote to a challenging work conversation, as well as how you'll position yourself, will vary, depending on how you foresee your relationship unfolding. If you're looking to build a stronger relationship with the person you are speaking with, you'll most likely be willing to put in the time and effort required to achieve consensus. If you're merely going through the steps that will allow you to end the relationship, you'll be brief and will choose your words carefully to avoid problems down the line should the employee decide to take this to HR, or worse, to a lawyer.

Once you know what you want out of the relationship, the next step is to get laser-focused on the outcome(s) you wish to achieve *before* scheduling a meeting. If you know going in what you want coming out, you're more likely to get it.

I'm sure many of you have been in a similar situation as Ron. You begin a conversation intending to go down one path and wind up on another. In Ron's case, commitment and presence weren't really what he was going after. These were underlying symptoms that were pointing to a bigger problem—lack of follow-up, which was negatively impacting the team and the hospital.

I've known Ron for years, and he's not a guy who minces words. Had Ron been more exact on the behavior change this employee needed to make *before* conversing with the employee, he would have been more explicit when addressing the situation. He's a great leader, and I have no doubt that he will use this opportunity as a learning experience. He's not going to make this same mistake twice.

Here are some questions to help you become crystal clear on your objectives before addressing a sticky work situation.

What's the Purpose of This Conversation?

Are you looking to blow off steam, or do you genuinely want this relationship to improve? Do you want your boss to take notice of your contributions, or are you simply providing information? Is there a particular behavior you'd like your coworker to stop or start doing, or are you merely venting? Essential questions like these are often not given proper consideration, which is why many of these conversations go nowhere or somewhere unexpected.

Let's say someone's actions are impacting you in a negative way. You may have every right to be angry or disappointed. However, telling your boss, peer, or team member off could result in unintended consequences. Before taking this approach, think about the damage you may do to your relationship or even your career. Then, if at all possible, choose a different path.

What Specifically Do I Want the Other Person to Do after Our Discussion Ends?

Have you ever been to one of those meetings where the person leading the meeting spent most of the time going down their list of items they were unhappy about yet never explicitly stated what they expected to happen next? I have. These types of meetings can be maddening. If you're like me, you probably left scratching your head, wondering what precisely the purpose of that meeting was and what, if anything, you were supposed to do next.

Before asking someone to speak with you in what could be an uncomfortable conversation, establish what you want the person or people in the room to do when they leave that meeting. When you're clear on the next step, you may choose a different course of action than what you initially thought you'd do.

Here's what I mean by this. Let's say you've decided that you're not interested in hearing what people have to say about a particular situation. You merely want to give folks a status update and inform them that you're incredibly disappointed in the team's revenue numbers. There's no point in pulling people into a room just to hear you speak. You may be better off delivering your message in an email, where you can spell out exactly where things stand and what you expect going forward. If need be, you can then schedule one-on-one meetings for those who desire clarification.

What, if Anything, Am I Willing to Commit to in Order to Get the Results I'm Seeking to Achieve?

If you look back at some of the more uncomfortable conversations you've initiated, you may notice a pattern. Maybe you're one of those people who look the other way more often than you should. Or perhaps the only time you provide feedback is when you've gotten to the point where you can no longer be silent. Or possibly you weren't clear on how you wanted to be treated, and now you're finally ready to take a stand. All of these situations may require you to commit to behavioral changes so you can get the results you're seeking.

Let's say that you recognize that you're part of the problem. Before proceeding, jot down what you are willing to commit to doing differently in order to get the results you need. For example, suppose you're one of those people who hates confrontation. You'll look the other way or pretend things are okay, until things are so bad that you no longer have a choice. You've reached the point where you've decided today is that day you are going to say something.

In situations like the ones I've described, to ensure you get what you need from this conversation, you must be willing to acknowledge the part you may have played that has gotten you to this point. You'll want to assure the other person that you'll be more forthright in the future. You can do this by promising that from this point forward, you'll let them know immediately when something is wrong. You'll no longer wait days (or months) before bringing matters to their attention. Ask them to do the same. Tell them if they feel you're not honoring your promise, to immediately let you know. As the conversation comes to an end, ask what else the other party needs from you to move forward together.

How Does Your Goal Stack Up with Your Counterpart's Objectives?

If you both have a common goal, you'll more than likely be able to move forward together more quickly. See if you can uncover a shared goal that will help you frame your conversation in a way that will get you positive results.

Let's say your manager has told you time and time again how valuable you are to her. You've been waiting patiently for a long overdue promotion and feel it's time to make a move. You both have a shared goal—your manager would like to retain you, and you'd like to remain with the firm. With this in mind, you can say to your boss, "I don't want you to think that I'm not excited about working for you because I absolutely am. At the same time, if I continue to remain in this job, I wouldn't respect myself, and I don't think you would either. Let's talk about the leadership position you mentioned and the timeline for me moving into that role."

Now let's look at what might happen in this situation if you discover that you *don't* have a shared goal. Your manager wants you to remain in her department, as you're someone who would be hard to replace. You're ready to move on.

Neither of you see eye-to-eye. Your manager wants you to stay under her supervision, and you wish to work for someone new. The conversation you need to have is one where you demonstrate to your boss why it's in her self-interest to help you secure that promotion. I say this because people act based on emotion. When people see what's in it for them, they're more likely to say yes to a request.

With that in mind, you have to convince your manager that helping you get promoted will reflect on her kindly. You could point out that she'll have a line of people waiting outside her door, all wanting to work with her when word gets out that she's *the* leader to work for, if you're going to move up in this organization. Senior management will take notice, which will provide her with more respect in the organization and access to more resources. Or, of course, you can always take the approach of saying nothing and remaining in a position that's no longer challenging or looking for a job outside the company.

The Four Factors to Consider When Preparing for a Difficult Conversation

Factor Number One: Your Relationship to the Other Party

We touched upon this topic briefly. Given that your relationship to the person you are interacting with is a critical factor in conducting a conversation of any kind, it only makes sense to do a deeper dive into this subject.

How you approach and conduct a conversation with someone is entirely dependent on the relationship you have or don't have with the person you're speaking with. It would stand to reason that the way you would approach someone you've known for years would be very different than someone you met for the first time last week. Say you've attended graduate school with a coworker, and you've worked off and on together for several years. Experience tells you that this person doesn't react well to surprises. Before having "the big talk," you know that you better have spoken about the topic at hand (more than once), or this individual will not react kindly.

Now suppose the employee you need to speak with is someone you met for the first time last week. In this case, you'd want to broach the topic that's weighing on your mind carefully. It would help if you thought through what you might do if the conversation doesn't go as well as you hope, and how you might respond should things go better than expected.

Factor Number Two: Preferred Communication Style of the Other Party

A ton has been written on the topic of preferred communication style in the workplace. Why? Because being able to quickly identify someone's preferred communication style will allow you to adjust your approach as needed. Those who can readily decode the communication preferences of the people they speak with fare far better in conversations than those who don't.

I'm seeing this play out right now with one of my clients, who, like me, is very direct. Her "New York" style, as we jokingly call it (hey,

I'm from New York so I can say this!), is impacting her ability to build strong relationships with her peers, who tend to be more casual and indirect ("Californian") in their communication style. Her teammates prefer to have a few minutes of chit-chat before jumping into what's on the schedule in their high-powered senior leadership meetings, especially when they know the day's schedule will be trying. She, on the other hand, gets right down to business as soon as the meeting is called to order.

My client has learned the hard way that her "let's just get this done" approach is doing more harm than good. I've suggested that she divide her most frequently called upon contacts into four categories, which are listed in Table 2.1. Keep in mind that most people won't fall perfectly into one of these boxes, nor does everyone in a particular category possess all traits. This chart is meant to be merely be a guide you can use to quickly assess someone's style and adapt yours accordingly.

This guide will help prevent you from making the mistake of trying to make small talk with someone who doesn't want to or refusing to do so with someone who does. It's one thing to refuse to adjust in a social setting, but it's another to do so when your livelihood depends on it. As a bonus, if you invest time to understand how others might act and respond, you'll be able to shorten the relationship-building cycle.

Let's look at one of the most talked about four-quadrant behavioral models, which the popular DISC assessments are based on. This social-style model is based on the research of William Moulton Marston. According to Marston, people generally fall into one of the four social styles shown in Table 2.1. The way they react in certain situations will depend on a number of factors, including the amount of stress they're under and how the person they're interacting with comes across in conversation.

Your ability to quickly identify and adapt your style to the other party's preferences will have a direct impact on your ability to build a relationship that can handle uncomfortable interactions.

Here are some examples of when and how you might need to make adjustments based on the other party's communication preferences.

TABLE 2.1   SOCIAL STYLES

Driver	Amiable	Expressive	Analytical
Highly conscious of time	Relationship-driven	Highly verbal	Logical
Goal-oriented	Supportive	Big-picture focus	Likes data and facts
Results-driven	Enjoys building consensus	Low attention to detail	Process-driven
Deadline-oriented	Cares deeply about people	Competitive-ambitious	Organized
Seeks to achieve goals rapidly	Cooperates to gain agreement	Desires to be accepted by others	Focused on tasks
Decisive	Respectful	Talkative	Detail-oriented
Strong-willed	Agreeable	Likes recognition	Skeptical

- If you're dealing with a driver, avoid chit-chat. But if you're with an expressive, be prepared for lengthy digressions.

- A conversation with a driver should be short and to the point, whereas when speaking with an amiable, trust is essential and small talk is welcome.

- Provide an analytical with the facts. Give a driver a quick synopsis.

- When providing an expressive with negative feedback, acknowledge positive points before discussing areas where this person may be failing.

- Don't try and move an amiable toward a decision until you've gained conceptual agreement with them. Be prepared for an expressive to agree with you on the surface, as their desire to be accepted by others may prevent them from immediately saying what they're really thinking.

- Drivers make decisions, so be prepared for them to say (early on in the conversation), "Okay, I can do what you're asking." Analyticals will want time to examine all the facts, which may require a second meeting.

- When speaking with analyticals, use examples and supporting evidence to back up your statements. Drivers will want to get straight to the punch line.

- Expressives and amiables will want to talk about how you got here, while drivers couldn't care less. They simply want to know where to go from here.

With practice, you'll get better at identifying the preferred style of the person you're speaking with and how you can best adapt. Eventually, this will become second nature.

Factor Number Three: Timing

Have you ever noticed how some people have impeccable timing while others seem to be oblivious as to what's going on around them? I have. Take the example of an employee asking for a raise ten minutes after the company announces a significant drop in earnings. Or the boss that comes into your office on a Friday at 5:00 p.m., sees you packing up for the weekend, and begins a discussion that you know is going to go well into the evening hours.

There's a time and place for everything, including the handling of challenging conversations. We'll get to place in a moment. When deciding the best time to take on a situation, think less about yourself and more about the person you'll be addressing. Let's say you're disappointed with how your boss handled a particular matter. You've made the decision that you are going to speak up and express your dismay. You check your manager's schedule and see he will be in back-to-back meetings until 2:00 p.m. Anxious to get the conversation over with, you grab the 2:00 p.m. time slot.

I can pretty much predict how this conversation is going to go based on your timing. Your boss will be distracted as he thinks about how he's going to get to all the calls and emails that are now waiting for him. He may even be feeling a bit exhausted, having just attended a string of endless meetings. This is *not* the time to say what's on your mind. Do yourself a favor. Look for an appointment time when your manager's schedule is less frantic. You'll be glad you did.

When it comes to effective communication, timing is a two-way street. If your boss or a coworker stops by and asks you if you've got a second to talk about an important matter, and you don't, you're best off letting the other person know this isn't a good time. Simply say something like, "My sense is you have something very important that you want to discuss with me. I want to devote my full attention to you, which I can't do at this very moment. Can we reconvene later on in the day or first thing tomorrow morning?"

When it comes to timing, we tend to underestimate how much time is needed to address delicate matters. Take those dreaded "I have to let you go" conversations. You go in thinking that you'll deliver the news, the person will take a few moments to absorb what you've just said, maybe they'll ask a few questions, and they'll be out the door in no time. Thirty minutes should be fine, right?

That's not how these discussions typically go. You may have had time to prepare yourself for what is, no doubt, one of the most challenging conversations any manager may have. However, the person on the receiving end of this news has just had his or her life turned completely upside down. They may very well need more than the thirty minutes you've allocated on your calendar. In situations like this one, you're best off booking more time than you think you'll need. I'm sure you'll have no problem finding something to do should you find yourself suddenly with a few spare minutes.

Factor Number Four: Location

We talked briefly about location. However, given how we work now and what work may look like in the future, this topic is one worth exploring more deeply. As noted earlier, where you hold a meeting matters as much as what you plan on saying. I've walked by conference rooms where it was obvious to me (and everyone else) that one of "those" types of conversations was taking place. I felt badly for the person sobbing in their chair and embarrassed for the other party, who didn't have enough sense to at least draw the blinds.

Finding private space these days isn't easy. The popular open office concept has resulted in droves of employees walking up and down the corridors looking for a quiet place to convene. It's no wonder that Starbucks seems to have become an extension of some people's offices.

I remember waiting in line for my latte at a Starbucks and overhearing a conversation I'm fairly certain wasn't meant for my ears. At the table beside me was a manager firing an employee. If I heard what he was saying, you could bet others did as well, as the tables at Starbucks are very close together. It took a lot of restraint not to walk over and give this manager a piece of my mind (along with a copy of one of my books on leadership). I will confess, I did snap a photo with my phone and considered sending the picture, along with a note reporting what I had observed and heard, to the head office. You see, the manager had a company badge on his shirt, which would have made it quite easy to locate his boss!

The coronavirus pandemic has changed forever the way we work. Before the pandemic, it was considered bad form to terminate an employee or ask your boss for a raise from afar. Now it's deemed to be acceptable to have these life-changing conversations over Zoom or by phone. As of this writing, there's no telling what the "new normal" will look like. However, one thing's for sure. Virtual workplace conversations will not be going away anytime soon, which will add more complexity to what used to be a simple decision in terms of location—"My office or yours?" Of course, circumstances outside of your control may dictate where you're to meet. If at all possible, face-to-face meetings in the same location are preferable for those heart-to-heart work conversations.

Planning for the Worst and Expecting the Best

There's no way to predict how a challenging conversation will go, which is why you need to plan for the worst and expect the best. This is the equivalent of mapping out an alternative route to ensure you get to an important meeting on time, on the off-chance your traditional way is bumper-to-bumper traffic. When planning out your meeting, make a list of all the possible twists and turns that may occur. This way you'll be prepared to respond to any objection that may come your way.

Here are four common scenarios you may encounter.

The Deflector

The person you're attempting to have a conversation with is superb at deflecting. In all likelihood, he'll do his best to drag others into the conversation so that he can shift the attention away from himself. He'll say things like, "Why are you singling me out? You never say anything when others come in late" or "Well, maybe my sales numbers haven't been great, but remember the time I volunteered to run the United Way campaign for our office?"

When dealing with deflectors, it's best to stick with the facts and stay on course. Be prepared to say things like, "We're not here to talk about your coworkers. We're here to discuss your excessive tardiness. In the past month, you've arrived at work well past your start time." Then be prepared to share the specific dates and times when these infractions occurred.

Sob Story Experts

These are the people who will have a sob story ready for every situation. These same individuals made the words "My dog ate my homework" famous. As soon as you begin to speak, they'll have a heart-wrenching reason as to why they're in this situation. Reasons may include "Things have been tough at home lately" or "My kid is being bullied in school." They're telling you this with the hope that you'll go soft on them.

Look, we're all human, and stuff does happen. Sometimes it's hard to separate fact from fiction. That's why I recommend you presume good intent. Acknowledge the difficulty the employee has shared. Then steer the conversation back to where you need it to go. Here's a brief script you can use or modify. "I'm sorry to hear your child is being bullied in school. I'm sure it must be stressful for you and your family. We still need to talk about..." followed by "Do you want to discuss this now, or should we reschedule for first thing in the morning?"

The Teary-Eyed Employee

The employee you are about to speak with is known to be highly emotional. Look at this employee the wrong way, and the tears will flow. Schedule extra time for this meeting, as no doubt you'll need to take a pause while the employee pulls him or herself together. You'll need to use some empathy here to move the conversation forward.

If the person you're meeting with begins to sniffle or cry, stop the meeting and ask, "Would you like a minute or two to compose yourself?" Get comfortable sitting there silently, while the other person collects themselves. When you get the sense that they're ready to hear what else you have to say, continue speaking.

Mr. or Ms. Non-Accountability

We all know people who take no responsibility for their actions. A few of these people may even work for you. When interacting with those who never take responsibility for their actions, it's advisable to have all your ducks in a row. Make sure you have your facts and figures easily accessible, as no doubt you'll be needing these items. The moment they realize you're about to call them out on their behavior, they'll say something like, "I have no idea what you're talking about," or "This has nothing to do with me. Why are you even talking to me about this?" You'll have to be strong here and say, "Actually, this most definitely has something to do with you," followed by "Here's what I mean," as you place Exhibit A on the table.

I've had times (although admittedly they were rare) when I was pleasantly surprised with how well a conversation that I was putting off went. I was expecting the worst, and then someone would say, "You're right. I haven't been giving it my all," or "I'm sorry if I came across as uncooperative. That really wasn't my intent. What do you need from me to fix this?"

I remember one such conversation, where I was completely caught off guard. One of my employees, whom we'll call Lila, pushed the limits with me daily. Every day, she had a different excuse as to why things weren't getting done. I was a young manager (age twenty-four) who did my best to cope with her shenanigans. One day, I finally decided I had had enough. I called her into my office and was prepared to read her the riot act. As I began to charge my way through the conversation, she stopped me and said, "Everything you're saying is true. I could give you a million reasons why I've made so many mistakes. I know I can do better." Lila had laid her sword down in front of me, which caught me off guard. I tossed aside the mile-long list in my hand of everything she had done wrong and allowed her to steer the conversation, which in retrospect, was a huge mistake.

Lila shared personal stories with me about her home life that had me feeling sorry for her. I felt so bad for her that I let her off the hook, which came back to bite me big time. Her behavior became more erratic, which reflected poorly on me. I spent the next several months figuring out a way to exit her out of the organization, but not before she could do additional damage to my reputation and hers.

If I could go back in time, I would have done things a lot differently. The moment Lila had taken responsibility for what she had done, I would have said, "Thank you. Now tell me, what are you willing to do to ensure this doesn't happen again?" I would have made a note of everything she committed to, had her sign the paper that I wrote it on, and let her know *exactly* what would happen next, if she could not keep her commitment.

The best-case scenario was right in front of me. Only at the time, I didn't know it and wasn't prepared when Lila didn't push back. As you get better at handling tough conversations, you'll be more open to the possibility that the conversation you've been dreading will go a lot better than you think it will. You'll get the timing down and will confidently say what needs to be said. You won't worry about being loved. Instead, you'll seek respect. I got there, and so will you.

Assessing Your Readiness to Proceed

We've talked a lot about the need to prepare. However, at some point, you have to stop planning and start doing. Here's a Conversation Readiness Assessment Tool you can use to determine if now is the time to take action.

TABLE 2.2   CONVERSATION READINESS ASSESSMENT

Rate each statement on a scale of 1 to 4	4 = Totally agree 3 = Agree 2 = Disagree 1 = Strongly disagree
I have a good sense of the preferred communication style of the other party.	☐
I've considered both worst- and best-case scenarios regarding how this conversation might go.	☐
I feel calm, centered, and able to address this situation.	☐
I have data and facts ready to share, should I need to do so.	☐
I'm ready to hear what the other person has to say.	☐
I trust myself enough to know that I will handle this conversation well.	☐
I have a trusting relationship with the person I'm about to speak with.	☐
I'm clear on the outcomes I want to achieve as a result of this conversation.	☐
I'm able to state specifically what I want the other person to do after our conversation ends.	☐
I know what I'm willing to commit to in order to get the results I'm seeking.	☐
I'm clear on what our common goals might be.	☐
I've given ample consideration as to whether or not the timing is right to have this discussion.	☐
I've selected a location for our meeting that feels appropriate, given the circumstances.	☐

SOURCE © Matuson Consulting, 2021. All Rights Reserved.
NOTE Any area with a score of 2 or lower requires immediate attention! Give these areas more consideration before proceeding.

Handling Difficult Conversations Remotely

No one could have accurately predicted that one day just about the entire world would go remote. But that's precisely what happened when the coronavirus hit and pretty much brought everyone to a standstill. Within days of the official announcement of a pandemic, employers shut down their offices and sent workers home, leaving no time to train leaders on how to best manage remote workers. As a result, managers were left to figure many things out on their own. This "experiment" went better for some managers than others.

Suddenly, it was no longer possible to meet someone face-to-face. We became experts on the use of Zoom and Microsoft Teams overnight. Video conferencing equipment, such as computer video cameras and ring lights, immediately sold out and were on backorder for months. People made do with what they had, which in some cases made it next to impossible to see someone's face when speaking to them. This was unfortunate, as you can tell a lot about how well a conversation is going based on visual cues. But what happens when you can no longer read a person's face because the lighting in their home office room isn't quite ready for prime time? Or a bad internet connection has them turning their video camera off and going into audio mode only? You learn quickly how to adapt.

As experienced leaders of remote workers know, the need to have difficult conversations with employees doesn't go away when employees are remote. The way you handle challenging remote interactions will ultimately reflect on you and the company. The last thing you want to do is be like Uber and make headlines for the wrong reasons. In May of 2020, Uber laid off over 3,000 employees in a three-minute Zoom call, which was recorded and shared globally by someone on the call. The backlash that occurred from this error in judgment was felt around the globe. I bring this up because learning what *not* to do in situations is just as important as learning best practices. Never lose sight of the fact that those you're engaging in conversation with are people who deserve to be treated with respect and compassion.

Avoid mass firings via Zoom or any other platform, and you'll be one step closer to doing things right. In fact—eliminate the practice of mass firings and you'll be that much further ahead than the competition in terms of being the kind of organization where people love to come to work and customers love to do business.

Lots of leaders have been working remotely for years now, which means we can learn a thing or two from their experience. Here are some things to consider that may be different than those in-person meetings you've grown accustomed to.

Consider the Place and Time Zones

During the pandemic, many people picked up and moved—some to different time zones. Companies quickly learned that a meeting normally set to begin at 9:00 a.m. ET no longer worked for folks on the West Coast. Before setting a time for what may be an awkward interaction, consider where the other person is located, and do your best to pick a time when they'll be able to fully focus their attention on the matter at hand.

Also, consider where the employee may be when you're having the conversation. With so many people working from home now, privacy is at a premium. An employee may be distracted if they've got a young child running around their house or a spouse working nearby and may not fully take in your message. Give them a heads up that what you're about to discuss is best said in privacy, so they can move to a quiet place if need be.

Request That Cameras Be On

Some people choose to leave their video cameras off, as they find looking at their own image to be distracting. However, there are certainly situations where cameras on works best. When setting up a meeting, be sure to let the other person know that you'd like the video conferencing feature to be on. This will help to avoid what could be an embarrassing situation—being asked to turn your camera on when you're not "camera ready."

Put Yourself in the Other Person's Shoes

While it may be easier for you to get things off your mind with a quick email, that may not be what's best for the person on the receiving end. While you're feeling relieved that you've gotten something off your chest, the other person is left to figure out what exactly your email means. Email can be easily misinterpreted. Think of all the wasted hours and undue stress that one email can cause. Then take your finger off the send button and, instead, schedule a time to speak or simply give the other person a call.

Keeping Your Cool When Things Heat Up

It's not easy to stay cool when things get heated in meetings or during difficult discussions, especially when one party is completely caught off guard by something the other person says. We've all been there. You're called into a meeting and raked over the coals for something you feel you didn't do. Or, someone pulls out a wildcard that changes the entire nature of the conversation. Tempers flare, voices rise, and we ultimately lose sight of the bigger picture. It's not uncommon to leave these kinds of meetings feeling disappointed and wishing you could have a do-over. How do you avoid getting in this situation in the first place with so much on the line?

Watch for Signs That You're at the Tipping Point

Everyone reacts to stress differently. When stressed, some people hold their breath while others can't catch their breath. Your heart rate may go up. Your face may turn red. Your voice may get louder or you may go silent.

Be mindful of how you're feeling, while also observing how the person you're speaking with is reacting. The other person may begin to sit back in their chair, fold their arms, and disengage. Or they may advance their body forward and start hurling angry remarks at you. Once the first punch has been thrown, you can expect there will be more. Before you know it, you've got a full-blown boxing match going on.

Mentally step out of the boxing ring for a moment and take a few minutes to allow each party time to catch their breath. When you sense things have calmed down enough to continue, go back into the ring, calmly recap where things stand, and do your best to move the conversation forward.

Avoid Taking Things Personally

Of course, this is easier said than done. However, if you're going to bring the temperature in the room down a notch, you'll need to remind yourself, "This isn't personal. This is strictly business." Don't jump to conclusions the moment someone confronts you. Give yourself time to process what's being said. Take a step back and try to see where the other person is coming from. In many cases, they really do have your best interest in mind.

I recall a friend sharing a story with me about the day she told a manager on her team that she needed to improve in some areas. This person's reaction threw my friend for a loop. The employee responded by saying that throughout her *entire* life (she was twenty-seven years old), no one *ever* told her she needed to get better at something, including her parents! Maybe you grew up in one of these households, where you could do no wrong, and you were pretty good at whatever you did. You might actually be as good as you think, but certainly we all have room for improvement. Or perhaps you believe you're so great because no one dared to tell you differently. If you're like my friend's employee and your boss has a similar conversation with you, be open to the possibility that there are indeed areas where, with a few tweaks, you could become even more exceptional than you are already.

If you're the person who's initiated the conversation, be prepared for the other person to say some things they probably don't mean. Most likely, they've been caught off guard and aren't thinking clearly. They will spout the first thing that comes to their mind, without regard to the impact this may have on your relationship. Give it a few days and hopefully things will calm down. Then see if you can clear the air and get your relationship back on track.

Be Respectful, Even When Faced with Disagreement

The reality is that you are not always going to agree with the people you work with. However, disagreement does not have to be disrespectful. It's okay to say, "Let's agree to disagree," which sure beats, "Are you crazy?" Saying things like, "I value your opinion, and in the past, have always considered your position. However, this time, I'm simply unable to agree with you," shows respect while also making it clear you're not going to change your position.

You could also agree on some points while standing firm on others. This will help to demonstrate that you respect what the other person has to say while also taking responsibility for whatever you've done that's led to this situation. For example, you could say, "Well, I could see why you might feel that way, and if I've left you with that impression, I apologize. I'll be more clear in my communication going forward."

Remind Yourself That Disagreements, When Managed Well, Can Lead to Lots of Positive Outcomes

Early in my career, I landed a position in one of the hottest companies in Houston. I wasn't on the job for more than a week, when I began to receive a slew of calls from every temp agency in town. Admittedly, I probably wasn't as nice to those calling to solicit my business as I could have been. If the truth be known, I was overwhelmed in my new job and their calls were only making matters worse.

One woman, in particular, was very persistent. Her name was Melanie. I guess she caught me on a good day, and I agreed to have lunch with her. During our lunch meeting she presented ideas that I didn't necessarily agree with, yet she continued her efforts to build a relationship with me. Years later, she told me that she went into her boss's office and flat out refused to work with me after our first meeting. Luckily for both of us, her boss told her to go back and get another appointment with me. I say lucky for us, as we figured out a way to work together and are still good friends today. This would never have happened had we not worked through our disagreements.

Here's the thing. Many people don't realize that friction is a good thing. It shows the other party is interested enough to engage in debate. Now compare this to what happens when someone agrees for the sake of agreeing. They're not engrossed in what you have to say. They're merely trying to get rid of you.

Disagreements at work can also lead to higher levels of work satisfaction, which may seem counterintuitive. Imagine working in an organization where you feel unable to disagree. You do whatever is asked of you, even if what you're doing makes no sense. You're a cog in a wheel and nothing more. Now compare this to working in an organization where workers are encouraged *and* rewarded to disagree respectfully. Some companies, like Amazon, actively seek out employees who have the courage to challenge the status quo. Encouraging new ideas and even dissent is essential to running an innovative workplace. These work environments provide much more stimulation than those places where you're asked to check your opinions at the front door.

Can You Hear Me Now?

Remember those annoying cell phone commercials where the actor kept shouting "Can you hear me now?" as he searched for a place to find a cellphone signal? That's exactly what many of these workplace conversations sound like to me—both parties shouting loudly with the hope that eventually the other person will pick up the signal and change their behavior.

How often have you said something that you thought was perfectly clear only to find out later that the receiver had taken it the wrong way? This happens a lot. Probably much more frequently than it should. That's because we're so busy thinking about what we are going to say that we give little thought, if any, to how our message will be received.

How people hear your message is completely dependent on their perspective, which is based on their life experiences. I mentioned that early in my career I had one of those "Can we talk?" meetings with my boss. As you may recall, the "talk" didn't go very well (at least from my perspective). That episode left me with the work version of post-traumatic stress syndrome, meaning that from that day forward I would quiver and think the worst whenever someone asked, "Can we talk?"

Oftentimes when I've had to have one of those heart-to-heart talks with a subordinate, someone has come before me and has had a similar conversation with that person. Of course, I had no way of knowing if they were traumatized by the experience like I was. But what I do know now is that someone's experience will certainly impact how they interpret what I'm saying. With that in mind, here are some things you can do to speak in a way that will get others to hear you loud and clear.

Be Direct in Your Communication

In an effort to spare someone's feelings, we wind up leaving them dazed and confused. Managers telling employees they need to change their attitude is a great example of indirect communication, which leaves people guessing. My first reaction when a client says this to me is, "What the heck does that mean?" and I have no doubt the employee who is being told this is thinking the same thing.

I then ask my client, "If they changed the way you wanted them to, what would that look like and feel like? What specifically would they be doing today that they weren't doing six months ago? What would you see or hear that would tell you they now have a much better attitude?"

I encourage them to be specific and name the actions that would indicate to them improvement has occurred. For example, in meetings the employee would acknowledge others' work and seek to build upon these ideas. He'd volunteer to take on tasks instead of waiting to be asked. The employee would smile more when talking with customers. The more specific you can be when telling the employee what you'd like to see in terms of behavior, the better. This way, the employee will be fully aware of the criteria you'll use to judge their progress.

Choose Your Words Carefully

Leaders often share with me what they've said when addressing tough work situations, and these conversations usually begin with something like, "So I said, you aren't doing what I need you to do." The use of the word "you" often results in the receiver immediately going into defense mode. Now imagine how this same conversation might go if the leader started with, "I haven't made myself clear." This would certainly pique the interest of the person on the other end of the conversation and would result in them being more receptive to what else you might have to say.

The former assigns the blame for the communication snafu on the listener, while the latter indicates that the fault lies with the initiator. This may seem like a small thing, but as you can see, it's not. One approach feels like a direct attack while the other comes across as someone who is willing to take some responsibility for the current situation. When discussing specific issues, again, refrain from using the word "you." Rather than saying, "You are leaving your coworkers holding the bag when you come in late," say, "The problem is, when you come in late, your coworkers have to pick up the slack." The first approach immediately puts the person on the defense, whereas the second approach allows them to clearly see how their behavior is impacting others and why it's important to correct this.

Stick to the Facts

Facts are hard to dispute, which is why you want to stick to the evidence on hand. Talk about observed behavior and avoid hearsay at all costs. Many people are masters at the art of deflection. If you introduce something that's not a fact, they'll go off on a tangent, which will pull you off track. For example, say you're a manager addressing a tardiness issue with one of your direct reports. If you say, "I've heard from several team members that you didn't get into the office until well past 9:00 a.m. on Wednesday and Thursday," you'll immediately open the door to one of those "Who told you that?" conversations.

Now, what if, instead, you shared your observations when addressing this situation? Saying something like, "The problem is you've come into work thirty minutes late again. I stopped by your office at 8:30 a.m. on Wednesday and Thursday, and you were not in." This statement is a fact that cannot be disputed, as you observed this.

Listen, Don't Assume

Lisa Larter, CEO and founder of the Lisa Larter Group, learned a valuable lesson on the importance of listening, the hard way. She shared with me how difficult it is to listen to someone else's point of view when you've already formed an opinion on the matter and the impact this had on her relationship with one of her key employees. This lesson is one that she will never forget.

I recently came out and said, "I'm sorry. I didn't believe you," to one of my key employees. And then, she cried. I was guilty of being the worst boss ever. The truth is, I didn't listen.

My employee is one of those people who is a slow thinker. She likes to have time to think deeply and process information before moving forward. She had been telling me she needed help to manage the volume of work she was responsible for, and I didn't believe her. I made some assumptions about her experience and thinking style and applied them to her leadership style, which was wrong. I thought we needed a manager with more multitasking experience: someone who has eyes in the back of their head, who loves to juggle balls, has a high sense of urgency, and thrives under the pressure of getting it all done.

Late last year, this employee came to me and asked if it was possible to change her role and work in a different area of the business instead. She felt her skills would be better put to use there. I agreed to her request and the opportunity to find someone new.

Then six months later, the manager I hired to replace her came to me and said, "I can't do this. There is too much work." She wanted to quit. It felt like déjà vu. She was telling me the exact same thing her predecessor said—except this time, I was listening. I knew I had to act fast if I was going to turn things around. I made immediate and significant changes in the business, hired extra people, and promoted someone to be her assistant so she had additional support. And then I did what I needed to do next.

I apologized to her predecessor. I told her that I failed to listen to her. I had made assumptions, and I was wrong. She 100 percent deserved to hear that from me.

Every single day, we let our bias, assumptions, opinions, and beliefs get in the way of listening—really listening to what other people are saying. We all need to listen better. This is a perfect example why.

And for the record, I adore the employee that I apologized to and am grateful she saw enough of the positives in my leadership style and in the work we do together to stick with our team. I thank her regularly for having more faith in my leadership than I deserved.

> Lisa Larter
> CEO and founder
> The Lisa Larter Group

Entering into a discussion when you've already made up your mind isn't good for either party. The problem with holding preconceived notions as true is that they can lead us to beliefs that are not always correct. Lisa's employee was doing everything short of sending up smoke signals to make her aware she was drowning in work, only Lisa wasn't able to hear this. And to make matters worse, she told her employee she didn't believe her. This is not something I'd advise you to say, unless you have solid evidence that an employee is lying to you and you hope they will quit on the spot.

If you find yourself in a similar situation, it's best to step back for a moment and process what's been said. Don't try to come up with an immediate response. Instead, actively listen. Seek to understand the complete message that's being communicated. Lisa wasn't actively listening to what her employee was saying. Here's what she should have said. "So, what I'm hearing you say is that you're feeling overwhelmed and that there is more work here than one person can handle. Is that correct?" By saying this, Lisa would have been validating her employee's feelings and demonstrating to this person she was listening intently and fully understood her position. This would have then allowed them to brainstorm some possible solutions.

Let's not kid ourselves. Lisa got lucky that her employee didn't bolt out the door the moment she questioned her work ethic. I know Lisa personally, and my guess is she had made a few deposits in the bank of trust account with this employee that allowed her to make this rather large withdrawal. Her apology may have brought her trust account close to where it was before making this misstep. Lisa is a quick learner and hopefully will not have to tap into her trust account with this employee ever again.

Why the Need to Be Right Can Bring about the Wrong Results

We all know people who always have to be right about everything. You know the kind. They always have to have the last word. They speak louder and faster than most, on the off chance you can't hear them or you may attempt to interrupt them. They don't stop pushing their point until their opponent tires and finally gives up. You may even be this person.

Going for "the win" in any difficult work conversation is never a good thing, as that's not the objective here. Remember, you can be 100 percent right and still come out on the wrong end of a conversation. What we're going for here is for both parties to feel heard and respected so that an agreement on next steps can occur. This is unlikely to happen if the conversation turns out to be one of those "winner takes all" situations.

So, what can you do if indeed this person is you? You can start by vowing to work on correcting this behavior. But first, you have to believe that it's in your best interest to change what you're currently doing. A look at how know-it-alls are commonly perceived may help you better understand the unintended consequences of your actions.

Know-it-alls aren't particularly well liked. Their reputation for stifling conversations and ideas makes people want to avoid them altogether. People who fall into the know-it-all category readily dismiss the ideas of others, which means you're probably missing out on a whole bunch of learning opportunities. We can all benefit from hearing other perspectives—that is, if we're open to the idea that someone else may know a bit more about a particular topic than we do. People who are know-it-alls rarely stop and say thank you or even realize others have contributed to their success. As a result, they're often viewed as pompous and are hardly ever selected by others to work on high-profile team projects. You may be missing out on some great opportunities, which could catapult your career. Thinking you know it all can also put you in harm's way. Let's say you're on a slippery mountainside and about to fall off. No one is going to warn you. I mean, why would they? They'll just assume, since you have all the answers, surely you know you are about to go over the cliff.

Hopefully, I've convinced you to reconsider your ways. If so, here's how you can begin to rein in your behavior.

Stop Spouting Off Every Random Tidbit That You've Gathered on the Topic at Hand

Doing this will only make people not want to talk to you. Useless facts, are just that—useless. Adding more information to an already contentious conversation will do nothing more than fuel the flames. Believe it or not, in these situations, less is more. Select the one piece of information that best supports your position and then allow the other person to have their say.

Remove the Words "Actually" and "Obviously" from Your Vocabulary

Every time you start a sentence with the word "actually" or "obviously," you come across as someone who is about to teach someone else a lesson. Or worse, a person who clearly thinks they are better than everyone else. You've probably heard the phrase "Actually, that's not how we do things here" at least a dozen times. What's your initial response when someone says this to you? If you're like me, you do all you can to resist responding with a snarky comment of your own. You also want to avoid starting sentences with the word "obviously" as well, as this word can be misinterpreted by the listener. Here's what I mean. Let's say one of your employees has presented an alternative way of doing something. You're not keen on his idea, so you begin by saying, "Obviously, we're not going to go in this direction." This sounds condescending. Heck, if it were obvious to the person on the receiving end of this message, he would have never suggested it in the first place! Do this enough times, and you can bet this employee will not be offering up his ideas in the future.

Know Your Audience

As discussed earlier, some people love to engage in chit chat while others hate it. Before providing tons of additional information, ask yourself the following question. "Does anyone in this conversation care about what I'm about to say?" If you even *think* the answer might be no, then refrain from saying more, unless asked to expand on your idea. I can tell you from experience that holding back from providing additional information is extremely challenging for people who think they're the smartest person in the room. However, with enough practice, I'm confident you'll be able to get to a place where others will actually look forward to hearing what you have to say.

Think Twice before Correcting Someone

Sometimes people are wrong. But not every wrong thing someone says needs correcting. If you've ever helped your kid with their math homework, then you know that oftentimes there is more than one way to approach a problem. You're working side by side with your child to solve a math problem. You both get the same answer, only you feel your kid has gone about it all wrong because their approach is different. The first few times you try to show them the "right" way to do things they say, "That's not how we do it in school." Eventually you realize that what matters most is that your child knows how to solve the problem. Think about this the next time you're tempted to correct a team member who comes up with a great solution, even though you would have taken a different approach to come up with the same answer.

Naturally there will be times when you'll absolutely have to call someone out when they're wrong. A good way to begin a conversation like this is to start with a question. A simple "Where did you hear that?" or "That's really interesting. Can you point me to the data that supports this?" will help to set the stage for a meaningful discussion and will allow you to point out areas that are simply incorrect. I have found that when I've taken this approach, the other party usually comes to their own realization that they've made an error. Of course, for this to happen, you need to be sure you are indeed correct.

In the next chapter, we'll be talking about the third principle, compassion—something we can all use a little more of. Empathy and understanding go a long way when discussing sensitive work topics. Read on to learn how to tap into your inner self and show understanding when you encounter situations that call for compassion.

KEY LEARNING POINTS

- The success of any challenging conversation will be decided long before the conversation starts, which is why you need to first come to terms with what you want for the relationship.

- Get laser-focused on the outcome(s) you wish to achieve *before* scheduling a meeting. If you know going in what you want coming out, you're more likely to get it.

- There's no way to predict how a challenging conversation will go, which is why you need to plan for the worst and expect the best.

- There may be times when a difficult conversation goes better than expected, which is why you need to be prepared to accept this small win and take the conversation over the finish line.

- We've talked a lot about the need to prepare. However, at some point, you have to stop planning and start doing.

- Disagreements, when managed well, can lead to lots of positive outcomes, including improved relationships with work associates, who may later become friends.

- Friction is a good thing. It shows the other party is interested enough to engage in debate.

- How people hear your message is completely dependent on their perspective, which is based on their life experiences.

- If you want others to hear you loud and clear, be direct in your communication, choose your words carefully, and stick to the facts.

- Enter all discussions with an open mind. When someone tells you something, park your assumptions so you can listen deeply.

- You can be 100 percent right and still come out on the wrong end of a conversation. Keep this in mind the next time you find yourself going for "the win."

03

Compassion

Be Empathetic and Understanding

Suppose you've done the work, and you've established a trusting relationship with the other party. In that case, the person you're speaking with may reveal something else is going on behind the scenes contributing to the situation at hand. When this is brought to light, some people will quickly dismiss anything that isn't business-related as irrelevant—which is a mistake. People bring their whole selves to work, which means it's next to impossible to separate their business lives from their personal lives.

Acknowledging that someone may be going through a difficult time demonstrates to the other person that you are not just concerned about work—you also care about them as a person. People who feel cared for are more apt to openly discuss a difficult topic than those who feel no connection to the person addressing them, which is why I've selected compassion as one of the seven principles. To demonstrate compassion, you have to build rapport, which I'll show you how to do in this chapter. It's also essential to understand the role that body language plays in communication, especially when expressing compassion. I'll explain why you may want to slow down (and how to do so) in order to speed up the conversation, why you need to be fully present, and the role that silence plays in addressing challenging discussions. I'll be closing out the chapter with a discussion on hyper-empathy—a common trait that many people seem to have.

The Need for Compassion and Empathy

Early in my career, I was a very young leader (age twenty-four) who was responsible for a team of people who were much further along in life than I. Soon after I was promoted, several of my employees called out to care for sick children. That move was completely foreign to me, as I was both single and childless. When this happened, I remember thinking, "What the heck is wrong with these people? Don't they have a backup childcare plan for situations like this?" I now know while I was thinking this, my staff was most likely thinking, "How am I going to pay my bills? I don't have any sick pay left." Rather than telling my employees not to worry about things while they were home with their child, I'd remind them of deadlines that were looming on the horizon, not a move I'd recommend others follow. In retrospect, I could have and should have been more sympathetic.

It took getting married and having my own kids to truly understood that young children get sick—a lot. I've since learned a great deal about compassion and the importance of seeing the world through someone else's eyes. Unfortunately for the people who reported to me early in my career, this lesson came a bit too late. I tried to make amends years later in an article that I wrote titled, "Confessions of a First-Time Boss: An Apology," where I apologized for my behavior as a first-time leader. One of my former employees read the piece and wrote to me and said, "You really weren't that bad." I might have believed her had she left out the word "that." In sharing the lessons that follow, I hope you will avoid making similar mistakes to the ones that I and others have made.

Being empathetic is one trait that some people think you're either born with or you're not. I'm not one of those people, as I believe empathy is a skill that can be learned. For our purposes here, I'm defining empathy as the capacity to understand or feel what another person may be experiencing—in other words, being able to put yourself in someone else's shoes, even if you've never actually been in a similar situation. It's vital to master this skill in the workplace, as empathy promotes compassion, which leads us to actions that result in a more engaged workforce.

Empathy is a potent ability that can be especially useful when you're in a difficult conversation, as it will allow you to understand better how someone might react to what you're about to say. When you have more insight into how someone else may feel, you're better prepared to respond to whatever may come your way. I know there have been times in my life where I've paused in the middle of a heated discussion and thought to myself, "Is there something else going on here?" I've even gone so far as to ask the other person this question while watching my tone to ensure that I wasn't coming across as hostile. By expressing concern and compassion, I've been able to shift the conversation from adversarial to two people looking for common ground.

Sales executive Matt Androski experienced firsthand what happens when you're so anxious to complete a challenging work conversation that you miss the opportunity to show compassion for someone whom you care about. Here's his story.

Having difficult conversations with employees can be challenging. I usually go into these conversations with an open mind.

I once had a conversation with an employee years ago about her performance in her job. I saw her having many talents. She was hired to be a field marketing representative for one of my regions. She was very good, understood the technology, and was sharp around the technical side of our complex solution. After many months on the job, I promoted her to a field engineer. I wanted to provide her an opportunity to expand her role inside the organization. After that promotion, we promoted her to a direct sales account role to cover a territory.

After performing in her new role for many months, I received feedback from the sales team that she wasn't quite up to the task at hand. They asked that I sit down with her to discuss her job performance. Because I took an interest in placing her in the role, I felt responsible for discussing this with her. I wanted to provide her with the opportunity to succeed. To make matters even more challenging, I was also asked to address a personal relationship that she was having with another field rep.

I planned out the conversation that I was going to have and was intent on being straight, open, and honest with her. I started the conversation by saying, "I know you can do this job, but you're falling short in some key areas, which is negatively impacting the team. Frankly, I'm surprised you are struggling." I then said in a stern voice, "You need to get your head back in the game." As soon as I said this, I knew something was terribly wrong. She looked at me, with anger in her eyes, and said, "I have so many balls in the air right now that I don't even know which game I'm playing. One of my parents took ill and I'm now the primary caregiver." I said, "I'm very sorry to hear about your family member. I'd like you to work with your direct manager to see how you can have your territory covered should you step away." And then, without missing a beat, I said, "We need to talk about your relationship with your coworker." At which point, she shut completely down.

Matt Androski
Sales Executive

Matt entered the conversation with good intent. He genuinely wanted this employee to succeed. His commitment to being honest with his employee was refreshing, as too many leaders beat around the bush and often refrain from saying what *truly* needs to be said. He showed empathy when he said he was sorry to hear about her ill parent. However, he wiped out any points he may have scored when he immediately shifted the conversation to a personal relationship she was having with a coworker. He had delivered enough bad news for one day, and now that he knew the employee was struggling with some personal issues, he should have tabled this part of the conversation for another day. Doing this would have been the compassionate thing to do. He could have suggested that they reconvene in a day or two to pick up where they left off. Had he done this, she may have been ready to hear what he had to say about his concerns regarding dating a coworker.

Putting Yourself in Someone Else's Shoes

What I find so interesting about compassion, empathy, and challenging talks is that when we're on the receiving end of a difficult conversation, we'd very much like the other person to put themselves in our shoes and to be more compassionate. Yet, when we're the one leading such conversations, we rarely think about what else might be going on with the person we're speaking with. This happens for several reasons. The first reason is because we let our egos take control of the situation. Sometimes we're so focused on being right that we don't allow ourselves to consider that perhaps we got this one wrong and that there may be more to this story than we know.

Being more empathetic will require that you put your ego on pause, so you can pay attention to what the other person is saying without judgment. Let's look at an example of how your ego can sometimes get in the way and cause a conversation to go from bad to worse, and what you can do to prevent this from happening.

Imagine your colleague stops by your office and claims that important data is missing from the report you prepared. He's a bit agitated and even accuses you of leaving this information out on purpose. You're fairly certain the information is in the report. Your ego is shouting, "Back off, dude. How dare you challenge my work ethic?" You do your best to hold your tongue. But then he says, "I can't believe you call this quality work. What am I supposed to do with this incomplete report?"

At this point your ego comes off of pause. You take the report out of his hand, find the information he says is missing and you say in a snarky voice, "Maybe if you took the time to read the entire report, you'd see the information is right here."

Clearly your response was lacking in empathy. You may not have liked each other much before this conversation, and surely even less so after it was done. Now let's take a look at how this scenario might have unfolded had you successfully tucked your ego aside and shown some compassion.

No one likes being accused of shoddy workmanship. However, if you're seeking to preserve the relationship, you could have said, "Sounds like you're pretty upset. Let's see if we can figure out where we might have gotten our wires crossed." Upon finding the information he was seeking, you might have said, "Oh, here it is. I can see why you might have missed it. It's in the appendix. I've made this very same mistake myself."

This response demonstrates to the other person that you're sympathetic to what's going on with him. He's obviously upset, which you're acknowledging. Rather than getting down to his level and slinging harsh words back at him, you're attempting to move the conversation toward a cohesive resolution. By admitting that you have also made this mistake, you're indicating to him that you have a good sense of how he must be feeling right now.

The second reason we don't consider how the other person may be feeling has to do with the stories we often tell ourselves, both about ourselves and those involved. If we have to let someone go, we may say to ourselves how supportive we've been and how indifferent the employee has been. We may even go further and try to psychoanalyze the situation. We think about how hard we worked when we were in their position and then easily dismiss someone's unwillingness to do the same as laziness. This second reason is especially true for me.

In my first job out of college, I worked in HR for a major retailer, where I put in way more than forty hours a week. I'd stay late when needed and would come in on weekends without being asked. It was what we did in those days. Of course, times change, only I didn't get the memo. Some years ago, there was this big push for something called work-life balance. Honestly, it took a lot for me to wrap my head around this concept, as it was foreign to me. For a long time, I thought if someone didn't put in a sixty-hour work week, they were lazy. I mean, how can you be expected to be empathetic when an employee comes to you and tells you they can't get all their work done on time when they aren't willing to put in an additional twenty hours a week to do so? That was the sort of crazy thinking that took place in my mind. Eventually, I came around. This shift happened when some of my younger employees showed me they could get all their work done (and then some) and still make it to yoga class on time!

When we let our biases enter the conversation, we become defensive, angry, and resentful. This happens before either party says a word. We also miss an opportunity to see if we may have contributed to the situation and where we might need to improve. A way to release your biases is to presume good intent, which I still have to remind myself to do from time to time. Forget the stories you have in your head. Your experiences have nothing to do with the situation in front of you. I can almost guarantee you that the person you're having an issue with didn't wake up this morning and say, "Now, how can I make my coworker frustrated today?" You'll feel more engaged and less exasperated if you can view the other person as sensible and rational, rather than someone who is here to make your life miserable.

The Art of Building Rapport

Have you ever been faced with having to have a critical conversation with someone with whom you had little or no rapport? Maybe your predecessor left you with an employee with a performance problem, or you had to provide more oversight than usual to a newly hired employee. Or perhaps your situation was similar to the story that I shared with you about newly assigned employees calling in sick.

In retrospect, when my employees called in sick, I had an opportunity to build rapport with my new team, and I blew it. If I had shown some compassion, my people might have been willing to jump in and help me out when I needed an extra pair of hands, without me having to ask. Instead, they came to work, did their jobs, and went home, while I spent many a late night at the office by myself.

Had I taken a moment to ask a few questions, I may have had a better understanding of what my employees were going through, even if I had never actually been in their position. If I had done this, I'm reasonably sure I would have been more sympathetic and would not have been so abrupt. For example, when my employee called me at home to tell me she wasn't coming into the office, I could have shown concern by asking, "How are you doing?" followed by "Wow, I can't imagine what it must have been like to be up all night and still have to get up at 6:00 a.m. to care for your other child." I might have then asked, "Any idea how long you may be out?" followed by,

"I'm asking this, so I can determine if it makes sense to get a temp in here, so when you do return, you won't have a large backload of work waiting for you on your desk." I could have also come right out and asked, "How are you in terms of earned sick time?" If she told me it was an issue, I might have gone to my boss to see what options I could offer her.

Many people make the mistake of overlooking the value of building rapport. That's unfortunate, as communication and collaboration are so much more challenging than they have to be without it. For me, building rapport was especially hard when several of my employees were old enough to be my parent, and one was old enough to be my grandparent. We really didn't have a lot in common—at least I didn't think we did. Every year, the city I lived in hosted a livestock and rodeo show. This was a huge event that attracted the biggest names in country music. One day, one of my older employees asked me if I had plans for the weekend. I told her I was going to the rodeo to see Larry Gatlin and the Gatlin Brothers. To my surprise, she told me she was going as well. I then asked her who else she planned on seeing at the rodeo. Turns out that we had a number of musical artists that we both enjoyed. Our shared interest in music led to conversations that revealed we had more in common than I thought. I learned that if you dig deep enough, you'll find something that will help you connect, regardless of your differences. It's also important to note that rapport is the foundation of great working relationships. When you take the time to build rapport, you're signaling to the other person that you truly care about them. And when you understand what drives people, you'll know exactly what each person needs from you in order to have a meaningful conversation.

Can you recall when someone with whom you had no connection tried to give you feedback? How'd that work out? Most likely, you dismissed what they had to say without even considering that their observations might be valid. Now, think about when you had to give someone with whom you had a good connection some feedback. More than likely, this person was open to hearing what you had to say. Rapport makes others more receptive to accepting feedback and is essential, as feedback only works if someone is willing to listen to you.

A side benefit to taking the time to establish meaningful work connections means you have a better understanding of what drives people, which enables you to tailor your conversation with that person. Here's an example of how you can use this to your favor. Let's say you've worked for your present employer for several years, and you've reached the point where you're ready for a new challenge. You've wanted to discuss this with your boss for a while now. However, you haven't mustered up the courage to do so, even though you have a pretty good understanding of one another. An opportunity presents itself for you to make your desires known, and you take it.

During a recent Zoom call, your manager shares with you that he's working 24/7 since the merger went through. You respond by saying, "Wow, that must be hard on you and your family. I'm sure you wish you could make it to all of your son's football games, especially since this is his last year on the team." You then say, "You know, I may have a solution. In my previous company, I was the lead person responsible for integrating the operations after acquiring another company. What if you established a similar position here and moved me into it?" Your boss responds with, "That's an interesting idea. Tell me more about what you did in your previous company, as well as what you think you'd be comfortable taking on here."

I mentioned this earlier, but it bears repeating. People act based on emotion. Because you and your boss know each other reasonably well, you're able to empathize with him in terms of the challenge he is going through trying to balance work and his family's needs. He also felt comfortable enough with you to share the emotional toll this merger is having on him. You wouldn't be privy to this if all your conversations were strictly business. Your investment in building a good working relationship with your manager has made what could have been a tough conversation easy.

If building rapport were as simple as it sounds, everyone would be doing it. Let's face it, some people are better at small talk than others.

The good news is that all of us can improve our rapport-building skills. Some of the ways of building rapport are personal, so in some situations, it's better to do so in private meetings or when there's more time. For example, you heard through the grapevine that you and your boss share a common interest of both being computer geeks. You wouldn't necessarily want to blurt this out in a meeting, as this could be awkward. However, mentioning to your boss in your one-on-one meeting that you happen to game on the weekends could be a way to establish a connection.

Remember, when you understand what someone else is going through, it's a lot easier and more natural to be compassionate. As you take time to get to know the people whom you work with, you'll see that you have way more in common than you think. And who knows, you may even become one of those people who actually enjoys small talk.

Nonverbal Communication and Body Language

The key to success in professional relationships lies in your ability to communicate well. However, communication is not only about the spoken word; it's about your nonverbal cues or body language, which can speak louder than words. Body language is the use of mannerisms, expressions, and how we move our body that allows us to communicate without words. Whether you're aware of it or not, when you interact with others, you're giving off silent signals. Here's something that most people don't realize. These messages don't stop when you stop speaking.

Sometimes, when we are trying to be compassionate, we're saying the right things. However, our body language is saying something else. When what you say doesn't align with your body language, the listener will likely feel you're being dishonest. Being aware of your body language is especially crucial in creating a feeling of empathy because it is a significant part of the communication process. It's hard for someone to perceive you as being compassionate if they think you are lying.

How you communicate nonverbally affects how others see you, including whether or not they trust you. Since trust is needed in order to have any sort of productive conversation, it's important to consider the signals you may be unconsciously sending others. Because demonstrating compassion is often required for a successful outcome, it's worth spending some time to learn some ways to show compassion through body language.

Facial Expression

Have you ever had a conversation with someone who seemed to say all the right things, but their facial expressions were saying something completely different? Perhaps they told you they were extremely interested in hearing what you had to say, while at the same time, the look on their face indicated to you this wasn't the case. Or, you were pouring out your heart and you saw them roll their eyes. It's difficult to assess how you appear to others, without a mirror in front of your face. This is where having a trusted colleague or coach can be very beneficial.

When clients come to me for help on how to best handle a high-stakes situation they have to address, we often role-play. If we're doing this remotely, I always require our cameras to be on, so I can look for visual cues that may result in their message being misinterpreted. With their permission, I may even record the session so they can go back and review for themselves how they are coming across. If they plan on having a conversation using video technology, this approach is incredibly helpful, as sometimes we come across differently over video versus in-person meetings. If you don't have access to a coach, you may want to ask a trusted colleague or a friend to role-play with you. When doing so, be sure to provide direction in terms of the specific feedback you are seeking. And don't forget to ask for permission to record if you're practicing over video.

Keeping a poker face, especially when in the midst of a heated discussion, is a challenge for many. While you're waiting for your turn to reply, your facial muscles are working so hard that you may break out in a sweat. Here's a tip that I use in my coaching. If you're unable to look someone directly in the eye, because you know if you do, your face will tell them what you're really thinking, consider focusing your eyes just above the bridge of the other person's nose. To the other person, you'll appear to be looking directly at them when communicating, even if you're not. This move will also give you time to catch your breath, so you can return to the conversation more centered. I find that when people are nervous, they have less control over their facial muscles, which is why I always recommend scripting out what you want to say beforehand and practicing your delivery. Doing this will help you remain in control of your emotions and will help to ensure that the other person receives your message in the way you intended.

Posture

It always looks so cool when a character in a movie crosses their arms, leans across the table, and delivers their message in a forceful way. You just know the other person is going to do whatever is being asked, for fear they will face this person's wrath. This scene may work in Hollywood and land this person an Oscar. Unfortunately, moves like the one I just described don't quite work out the same in real life. Yet, we see people do this all the time. How you stand or sit conveys a strong message about how you feel.

If you want to come across as compassionate, then keep your arms uncrossed and lean slightly forward when listening. This will indicate to the other party that you're open to what they have to say and that you are listening intently. An occasional head nod, with a few words of acknowledgment, such as "I see," "Please go on," "I'm sorry to hear that," will go a long way to demonstrate compassion and understanding.

Voice

Have you ever had someone say to you, "I'm not angry!" in a voice that was so loud, someone had to come into the room to make sure you were okay? How you say something is just as important as what you say. When you speak, other people "read" into what you're saying by the tone of your voice. They are interpreting your timing and pace, your tone and inflection, and of course how loud you speak, and are making judgments.

If you're looking to convey a feeling of compassion, then you're going to want to modulate your voice so that you come across as concerned and caring. Saying "Sorry to hear that your grandmother died," in a somewhat sarcastic voice, could convey that you don't believe what you've just been told. Perhaps the person telling you this appears to have more grandparents than humanly possible, as this conversation feels like a weekly event. However, with so many blended families, the death of another grandparent could very well be real, which is why it's best to err on the side of caution and respond with some concern in your voice. In general, a soothing voice will result in better work conversations as well as better outcomes.

Slow Down to Speed Up the Conversation

In today's high-speed business world, where workers are expected to get everything done, stat—all without missing a beat—it's no surprise that people are subscribing to what appears to be a version of speed dating in the workplace. Here's what I mean. You meet your new boss and within twenty-four hours, you're supposed to go from new employee to confidant. You're also supposed to be able to think three steps ahead of this person. Otherwise, you'll fall behind. You're then supposed to repeat this level of relationship building with the next person you meet. The pressure is enormous, and the expectations are often ridiculous. Everyone wants to get results quickly, no matter what the cost. However, the pursuit of short-term wins at a rapid pace comes at an expense.

It may seem counterintuitive, but the fastest way to move difficult work issues forward is to slow down and, if at all possible, take time to establish a relationship with the person you need to speak with. However, too many people feel taking the time to get to know someone in today's busy world is more of a luxury than a necessity.

It's not—here's why. When you have a reasonably good working relationship with someone, they are more apt to trust you. When people trust you, they'll share things with you that will allow you to move through difficult conversations more rapidly and with compassion.

My client Jan learned this the hard way. Jan, who leads a team of communications professionals for a pharmaceutical company, confessed to being a type A personality. Her drive to get things done left her little time for socializing. Therefore, she knew next to nothing about the lives of her employees outside of work. This came back to bite her, in a way she never expected.

One of her employees, who had done a pretty good job over the years, began to miss some critical deadlines. Jan knew she had to address the situation right away, so she called him into her office and said, "In the last two weeks, you've missed three deadlines. This has to stop." The employee looked shaken and was about to say something when Jan interrupted and said, "You do know there are dozens of people who would like your job." At this point, the employee resigned himself to the fact that it was better to say nothing than to risk another lashing. He said to Jan, "You're right. Here's my two-week notice." She later found out from another employee that this person's spouse had just asked for a divorce and threatened to take his kids away from him. She confessed to me that she felt awful.

Having a loved one leave isn't something you usually announce to people who are nothing more than business associates, which is what Jan felt like to him. Had she slowed down for just a moment, she would have realized her employee's behavior was out of the norm. Clearly, something was wrong. And if she had taken the time to get to know her employees and not merely said hello, she might have had an inkling that something was amiss at this guy's home. I know Jan well enough to say that if she had known one of her people was struggling with a personal matter, she would have been concerned and would have come across that way. Instead of coming across as stern, she may have said something like, "You know, this isn't like you. Is there something going on that you'd like to share with me?" This approach would have provided the opening needed to discuss a suitable plan forward that would have been satisfactory to both parties. Instead, she lost a precious employee.

Being Present

We seem to have a lot going on these days, which explains why our minds frequently wander to a different task while we're doing another. Multitasking may be fine when trying to figure out what you're going to make for dinner while assisting a young one with homework. However, not being fully present during a high-stakes conversation can result in doing more harm than good, which is why it's so important to slow down and focus on what's in front of you. Unfortunately, I witnessed firsthand what happens when you don't.

I remember being in the room when my boss had to let a long-term employee go. While delivering the news, she was shuffling papers on her desk as she looked for a file she needed for her next meeting. I couldn't help but notice the employee's reaction to this. He began to get agitated. Here he was being fired, and the person telling him this seemed more interested in locating a lost file than showing any compassion for the situation he was going through. I vowed never to make the same mistake. Conditions like this one are the very reason why I tell my clients that it's our behaviors that matter most—not our intentions. I'd like to believe my boss felt terrible for this guy, and she may have. However, her body language and her actions indeed said something different.

There are certain times of the day when our minds are clear and we're able to better focus on matters that are right in front of us, than at other times. This may vary from person to person. I try to tackle tough conversations at the start of my workday. This prevents me from spending countless hours second-guessing myself. However, I know others who need at least two cups of coffee, and a morning snack, to engage in any conversation. You may fall somewhere in between, or you may do your best work later on in the day. The point here is that the right time to hold a tough conversation is when *you* can be fully present.

Silence Is Golden

Years ago, when I was going through a tough time at work, a friend suggested that I try meditation. I quickly dismissed her idea. As I mentioned earlier, I'm from New York, and we New Yorkers talk and move fast. Unless I could meditate while running from one activity to another, I wasn't interested.

My job situation went from bad to worse, and I soon found myself calling my friend back and asking for an introduction to someone she thought could help me. She referred me to a woman who was affiliated with an ashram. Over the next several months, I spent two evenings a week with her, sitting cross-legged on the floor and chanting. We'd end each session with several minutes of silence, which felt *much* longer to me. I remember feeling very uncomfortable with the silence part. So much so that I would occasionally clear my throat and open one eye to see if I could get her to end the session early. It took a while, but I eventually got comfortable with the silence and now admit that I ultimately looked forward to this part of our time together.

Take it from me; it's not easy to quiet your mind and be comfortable with sitting in silence. However, getting comfortable with silence is well worth practicing. Here's why. Think about a recent conversation where you were negotiating with someone for something important to you. You said your piece, and then the room went silent. You were so uncomfortable with the silence that you jumped in and started actually to negotiate against yourself, which happens a lot more often than you think.

My client Trish, who works for a tech company, was given her manager's responsibilities when he departed the company but did not receive a change in title or pay. After eight months of taking on this new role, she finally decided it was time to ask her boss for a raise. She did all the right things prior to asking for an increase. She compiled a list of her significant accomplishments over the past eight months and conducted extensive research on what the market was paying others in her field. She told me she went into the meeting feeling confident that her boss would say yes to her request. Trish walked me through her conversation, which seemed to be going well—and then hesitated when she realized her fatal mistake. When she told her boss that she believed she was worth $10,000 more than what she was being paid, he became silent. She sat there for what felt like minutes and then blurted out, "Um, it's okay if you can only give me $5,000. I get that times are tough."

Her uncomfortableness with silence cost her dearly. Her boss quickly agreed to increase her pay by $5,000, which meant she was still being undercompensated. As Lisa Larter, whose story I shared with you earlier in this book, points out, some people are deep thinkers. My guess is, her boss was taking a few minutes to think about how to best respond. Had Trish waited out the silence, he very well might have agreed to her original request. Or he might have counter-offered with $7,000, and they could have settled somewhere in between. We can all learn from Trish and Lisa that silence isn't a bad thing. In fact, quietness can be a good thing.

One thing I do know for sure is that a few moments of silence is a heck of a lot better than an immediate "No!" Here's how to get more comfortable with dead air in the room to help you achieve a mutually beneficial solution. The next time there is a long pause in a conversation you're having, take a deep breath, and count to twenty. If the person still has not responded, gently ask, "Do you understand what I'm saying? Or do you need me to reframe this?" In most situations, the person will say something like, "I'm thinking about what you just said. Can you give me a minute to think through my response?"

Using silence as a tool means that you'll most likely end a difficult conversation with much better results. Silence allows both parties to calm down faster. In turn, you will both be more receptive to hearing what's been stated because you'll both be less reactionary and more focused on the ultimate goal—a much better outcome and an improved working relationship.

Here are some other things to consider as you work on becoming comfortable with silence:

1 Not every lull is due to a mistake made by someone. If a particularly profound point is made, the other person may want to pause and reflect on it for a moment before responding.

2   There are situations where silence is socially acceptable. Some examples of this are when someone shares some heartbreaking news with you or if someone has asked you to comment on a complicated situation they've been struggling with. You may immediately know the answer. However, you may choose to pause so as not to appear as if you haven't given the matter serious consideration.

3   Silence may provide you with the perfect exit strategy for ending a conversation. Before the silence goes on for too much longer, take charge and say something like, "Well, it looks like we're going to have to agree to disagree." Or, "I'll let you get back to what you were doing."

4   Silence may merely be a memory lapse. Your mind freezes up on you or you've lost your train of thought. If you're the one who has gone silent, you can make light of the situation by saying, "Darn, I can remember what I had for breakfast two days ago, but I can't remember what I was just going to say to you!"

5   Silence is often used as a negotiation tool. You've heard that saying, "He who talks first, loses." All you have to do is look at Trish's situation to know this is true. Use silence to your advantage. Remain quiet and let the other person speak first.

6   There is no one-size-fits-all approach in figuring out how long to let the silence stretch, but a good rule of thumb is to allow the silence to continue until the other party indicates they are ready to converse again.

7   If a high-stakes conversation is incredibly important and requires some resolution, you are best off not ending with silence. In these situations, you can say, "I know this has been a difficult conversation. Let's reconvene in a day or so to discuss where we go from here."

Hyper-empathy: Is There Such a Thing as Caring Too Much?

Up until recently, I thought there was no such thing as too much empathy—that is until Sue Bergamo shared her story with me. Sue and I met a number of years ago at an executive breakfast I was hosting. She's a lifelong learner and was kind enough to share her story here to help those of you who, like Sue, may suffer from having a little too much propensity to help.

Several years ago, I worked at a company and hired an engineer who started out enthusiastic, energized, and ready for any challenge. The resource worked as a part of a small team with diverse skill sets and locations across the globe. He took the lead on a major transformation project and seemed to be enjoying his work. The workflow was solid, and headway on a critical project was being made.

This individual was employed for about a year when he had twins. Rightfully so, he was overwhelmed from the beginning and, as a new parent, suddenly had to learn a whole new set of skills to take care of his new family. Having a baby is difficult, and having two children at once can be exhausting. The exhaustion started as soon as the twins came home. This individual was so tired that he became run-down, and as soon as one cold ended, another began. It became clear that after the family leave period, more time would be needed, so I suggested that he work from home for the next six months. I felt that this was a reasonable period to become acclimated to the new scenario and responsibilities. Weekly check-in meetings were scheduled, and things seemed to get off to a good start. While a flexible work arrangement was provided, we also agreed that the work would be completed on time.

Since the company was running out of office space due to high growth and the work from home arrangement was going well so, we extended it. He continued to be sick often, and while a few dates had slipped, this individual continued to work from home for another six months. About month ten, deadline dates started to slip more often. I now had to schedule daily check-in meetings to help keep him on track. This lasted for a while, and he was very apologetic about the events that were unfolding.

I remained empathetic to the situation but started to struggle with the constant need to provide direction and refocusing. Our conversations remained respectful, but I became adamant about delivering and being responsible for commitments. There were many times that work was rescheduled or given to another team member to finish. The situation came to a standstill when I needed to follow up on his ability to follow up on meetings, notes, work, documentation, etc. He was unprepared when asked to facilitate meetings and, on several occasions, couldn't remember what the meetings he requested were about. It was clear that he was no longer delivering or engaged, and the individual was told that the work from home situation needed to stop.

Coming back into the office, he worked for the first month, then things began to slide backward again. The final straw came when a small task that was not completed in six weeks had to be reassigned to another team member, who completed the job in a few hours.

Budgets were continually being adjusted, and IT was an area that typically had to give back. Shortly after the last noncompletion of activities occurred, I was asked to give back on the budget and put this individual on the slate to be let go.

In retrospect, I was too easy on this individual and did so because I sympathized with his plight. Offering a flexible work arrangement was the right thing to do, though I should have ended the deal shortly after the second incident happened.

Sue Bergamo
CIO and CISO
Episerver

I have to hand it to Sue. Her heart was in the right place. She handled the situation with empathy and compassion and did her best to help her direct report work through this difficult time. However, while doing so, she failed to hold this person accountable to his end of the bargain. As a result, this employee continued to take advantage of her kindness, which led to Sue facing some very tough challenges of her own.

Sue admits that she should have ended the deal shortly after the second incident. To do this, she would have needed to be more explicit in her dealings with this person. In addition to stating her expectations, Sue should have gone further and communicated to the other person *precisely* what would happen if she deviated from their agreement. This would have set Sue up nicely had she needed to have a follow-up conversation regarding this matter and would have allowed her to move things along rapidly Here's what Sue's follow-up response might have looked like:

Sue: Wow! It must be extremely challenging caring for twins while you're also trying to work full-time. I imagine it must be exhausting. As you know, our team relies upon your work to meet critical deadlines, which is why I wanted to talk to you today. Deadlines are slipping. We should talk about how we can restructure your work arrangements to give you some flexibility. If I can arrange for you to continue to work remotely, you'll be spending less time commuting, which will give you more time to focus on the work that needs to be done. What are your thoughts on this, and what other ideas do you have to resolve this problem?

In the second stage of the conversation, Sue might say, "Okay, so we've agreed that you'll work from home for the next six months, *contingent* upon you doing the following." Sue would then summarize what was agreed upon. She would then say, "Let me be clear. If you fail to keep our agreement, for any reason, you will be required to return to the office immediately. If you're unable to do so at that time, or if your work fails to improve, we may need to terminate our relationship. I hope we don't get to this place, but I feel it's vital for you to know exactly where things stand."

In this proposed conversation, Sue is empathetic, while at the same time, she is laying out the roadmap for future heart-to-hearts, should they be needed.

The next chapter is on curiosity and the power of inquisitiveness. When we're curious, we see things differently, which helps us resolve our differences. If you're the least bit curious as to what I mean, read on.

KEY LEARNING POINTS

- Empathy is the capacity to understand or feel what another person may be experiencing. This skill can be learned.
- Expressing concern and compassion can shift a challenging conversation from adversarial to two people looking for common ground.

- When you understand what someone else is going through, it's a lot easier and more natural to be compassionate.

- The key to success in professional relationships lies in your ability to communicate well. However, communication is not only about the spoken word; it's about your nonverbal cues or body language, which can speak louder than words.

- How you communicate nonverbally affects how others see you, including whether or not they trust you. Since trust is needed to have any productive conversation, it's essential to consider the signals you may be unconsciously sending others.

- When communicating with others, be mindful of your facial expressions, posture, and voice. Make sure all of these are in alignment with what you're trying to communicate.

- It may seem counterintuitive, but the fastest way to move difficult work issues forward is to slow down and, if at all possible, take time to establish a relationship with the person you need to speak with.

- It's important to be *fully* present when having a high-stakes conversation.

- Embrace silence. Silence is often a sign that someone is listening deeply and needs more time to process what's been said.

- There is such a thing as caring too much. When this happens, you can easily be taken advantage of by others.

04

Curiosity

Asking Questions Rather Than Shutting Down

Have you ever wondered what makes people tick? I ask myself this question all the time, along with a whole host of other questions, which is why I've chosen to include curiosity as the fourth pillar for handling difficult workplace conversations. Being curious and asking questions to learn more about a particular situation shows the other party that you're interested in what they have to say, which helps to move a conversation forward. In this chapter, I'll be discussing the power of inquisitiveness and how the use of the *right* questions can help you gain a better understanding of the complex situations you may be discussing. We'll explore why curiosity did not kill the cat and why curiosity is a good thing. I'll show you how you can become more inquisitive. We'll explore how to tap into your inner child and regain the curiosity that you innately had as a young child. We'll cover a topic that is rarely discussed—what you can do to ensure you're not stifling curiosity in others. I'll be providing conversation starters as well as inquisitive questions you can ask to keep the conversation flowing. We'll end this chapter by taking a deeper dive into the impact curiosity has on conversations and how to regain control when a conversation goes off track. Have I piqued your interest? Let's get curious.

The Power of Inquisitiveness

Growing up, I was one of those annoying kids who asked "Why?"—a lot! Of course, at the time, I didn't know that I was fine-tuning a skill that would prove to be extremely valuable throughout my life. I've always been curious, especially when it comes to people, which probably explains why my life's work is all about the human condition. When we are interested, we see things differently. For example, you may see things as black and white, whereas I see many different shades of gray. You may be satisfied when someone makes a brief statement, such as "Our company stock is going to soar." Not me. My natural inclination is to respond with, "Why do you say that?" My intent in asking a question like this is not to put someone on the spot. I genuinely want to know why they feel this way, as I'm interested in all things business, and I'm also interested in how others see the world. Curiosity, at its core, is all about noting and being drawn to things we find interesting. Think about it. When someone starts to talk about a topic you're incredibly interested in, your ears perk up. You begin to contribute to the conversation by asking a question or two, demonstrating to the other party that you share a keen interest in the topic. Being curious and asking questions is one of the quickest ways to cement a relationship with someone. That's because curious people take an interest in learning about others, and they intentionally try to keep interactions engaging.

Whenever I ask someone if they are curious, they almost always say yes. Yet, I find curiosity to be in short supply. So many people consider themselves to be curious because a vital part of their role at work involves asking questions. However, these questions are often scripted. Asking scripted questions is on the surface problem-solving. Yet, problem-solving should not be confused with genuine curiosity.

Think about the last time you called a customer service number for help. Did the person on the other end of the call give you the impression they were genuinely interested in coming up with a resolution that would result in you becoming a lifelong customer? Or were they merely going down their list of questions with little regard for your responses? I recently had a customer service experience that was less than satisfactory. We ordered patio furniture in June for our summer home that finally arrived in late August. When I opened up the boxes, I discovered that the chair pads were missing. I immediately put in a call into customer service, where the rep was reading from a script. No matter how hard I tried, she stuck to her script. She asked a few standard questions. However, she was unable to help me. I then had a more animated conversation with her supervisor, who asked me similar questions to the ones I had already answered. Eventually, she offered me a coupon for 10 percent off a future purchase. But she didn't ask me the one question that really mattered: "What can I do for you that would make you happy?" The situation went from bad to worse with promises for redelivery being made and more service failures. Eventually, I was able to speak to someone who had a bit more authority than the supervisor. Without me asking (or him asking what I wanted), he offered to take 50 percent off of my current purchase. I said, "Thank you," hung up the phone, and vowed never to do business with them again.

You may be wondering why I would quickly write off a company that was willing to do more for me than what I originally wanted. It's simple. Throughout this experience, I never felt genuinely cared for. I was left with the impression that I didn't matter. That's what happens when people aren't inquisitive. The other party leaves the conversation feeling uncared for, which is not at all what we're going for here. Don't make this same mistake. Be curious. Ask questions, and you may even learn that a problematic situation can be resolved with a lot less effort than you initially thought might be required.

Tapping into Your Inner Child

As adults, we generally believe that children learn a lot from us. That notion is correct because children see everything we do and absorb life lessons about how to behave. However, most of us haven't given much consideration to how much we can learn from children. For the most part, kids are relatively straightforward in their communication, which is an excellent lesson for all of us. When gathering stories for this book, I found that the most significant regret people had was not being direct in their communication. They acknowledged that their indirectness created a host of problems that could have easily been avoided had they not skirted around the issue.

Children are curious about the world and why things are the way they are. They are also curious about other people. Think about how many times as a child you pointed to someone while asking your parent a question about this person. Your parent probably told you it was impolite to point, while quickly changing the subject. You may have, like me, interpreted this to mean asking questions about other people is taboo, which may not be exactly what your parent was trying to teach you. Curiosity is a wonderful trait to have.

Have you lost your sense of curiosity? If you find yourself less curious now than when you were a younger version of yourself, keep reading this section to learn how to reignite your sense of wonderment. However, if you still believe you have retained your sense of curiosity, then you can skip ahead to the next section, Stop Stifling Curiosity in Others.

Children are also resilient and generally bounce back from stressful situations, which is an excellent reminder of how resilient we can be when faced with adversity. No doubt just the *idea* of having to have a difficult conversation with someone is stressful for most. If the thought of having to address an uncomfortable situation is making you anxious, try channeling your inner child. Think of a time when you were young, and you had to do something that made you extremely uncomfortable. At the time, you may have felt like you would never recover, but you did. And perhaps with some distance behind you, the situation wasn't nearly as bad as you made it out to be. Now, think of the case that's in front of you. In all likelihood, a few months from now, you'll look back on this and realize that what you had to handle wasn't as bad as you anticipated, especially if you incorporate many of the suggestions that are in this book.

Kids take lots of risks, which may help to explain all the scars and broken bones accumulated while attempting to master a new sport. When we're young, we seem to view our injuries as a badge of honor. Yet, as we mature, this is no longer the case. We tend to take fewer risks, as we fear we may not bounce back so quickly from an injury. I see a similar pattern in the workplace. Young leaders tend to take way more risks than mature leaders. They seem less fearful as to what may occur if they make a wrong move. In time, and with a few "What the heck were you thinking?" conversations with their boss, they grow more cautious, which is unfortunate. Many leaders ask themselves, "What will happen to me if I address this situation and I handle it wrong?" when instead they should be asking, "How will things be better off when I get this conversation right?" In my experience, the fear that holds people back from having courageous conversations does far more damage than what might happen in reality. If the truth is known, the only injury I've seen occur due to taking on a challenging work conversation is a damaged ego, which most people quickly recover from.

Kids take things way less seriously than adults and look at each day as a new venture. Adults, on the other hand, tend to focus on all the things that can possibly go wrong, which is something a child rarely considers. I'm not suggesting that you shouldn't give great care to a conversation you're about to have with your boss, coworker, or your employee. However, you may want to consider lightening up a bit. Whenever I appear to be devoting way too much time worrying about something, my mentor, Alan Weiss, always says, "What are you worried about? No one is shooting at you!" which is a great reminder that perhaps I'm overthinking things. Consider this the next time you're faced with a challenging situation and try to look at the situation as a learning experience—or as the kids would say, a new venture.

Young people live in the present without thinking about what's next on their plate. Oh, to be young again! When was the last time you lived in the moment? Most of us tend to get ahead of ourselves. Rather than looking at a complex situation and saying, "Okay, my first step is…" we tend to make things more complicated. "I'm going to say this and if he disagrees, I'll then say that. And if things get heated up, I'll then say…" You're so busy planning what you're going to say next as the conversation is unfolding that you aren't fully taking in what the other person is saying. As I mentioned earlier, it's certainly a good idea to be prepared for all possibilities and it's equally as important to be present. The next time you're in a deep conversation and you find yourself worrying about things that are yet to come, take a deep breath. Consciously listen to the person speaking by focusing on what they have to say. This will not only help you remain in the moment but will also help you strengthen your work relationships. When all else fails, try being as passionate about listening as you are about wanting to speak—an idea we can all benefit from.

Why Curiosity Didn't Kill the Cat

Most are familiar with the common proverb, "Curiosity killed the cat." In fact, you may have been told this by a parent or someone who meant well when you asked one too many questions. This cautionary expression was intended to serve as advice suggesting that it's best to mind your own business. Minding your own business might be great advice in some circumstances. However, there are certainly times when the need to be curious supersedes the worry associated with being considered a busybody.

Imagine if every time there was a tough situation at work that you knew needed to be addressed, you took the position of steering clear for fear the other person would find your questions to be intrusive. You'd never confront anyone about anything! You owe it to the other person (as well as yourself) to tackle tough situations when they come up, which is why I'm encouraging you to become more curious. Here's how to begin.

Start by participating in this brief exercise to test your curiosity quotient. Think about your position on a specific social issue and find someone who has the opposite opinion. Ask this person seven open-ended, nonjudgmental questions designed to help you understand their point of view. While doing so, give them no indication that you disagree with their position. You will know if you are coming across as curious if the other person becomes keen as they talk with you, an engaged listener. If you find this exercise nearly impossible to do, then the answer is clear... you're not as curious as you think. The good news is, curiosity skills can be improved with practice—that is if you're really interested in getting better at this, which I hope you are.

Curiosity is such an important skill and is necessary in order to have productive workplace conversations pertaining to difficult topics. No one will trust you until they feel you understand where they are coming from. Asking open-ended questions like, "How do you feel about…?" or "What solution do you think would be ideal in this situation?" helps you to build trust. There are a lot more questions where these came from. Here are ten open-ended questions you can use to show you're deeply interested in moving a difficult conversation forward. When proposing these questions, be mindful of your tone. Remember, this is a conversation—not an interrogation!

1 Could you help me to understand how we got here in the first place?

2 What would you see as the ideal solution?

3 What's your understanding of the problem?

4 Why do you think this happened?

5 How do you feel about the current situation?

6 Where do we go from here?

7 If you were me, how would you handle this situation?

8 What do you see being at stake here if nothing changes?

9 What's going through your head right now about this situation?

10 Now that you have this information, what do you plan to do?

Stop Stifling Curiosity in Others

Although most leaders would like to believe they value inquisitive minds, in reality, most stifle curiosity. Several of my coaching clients report to leaders who have told me that they'd like my client to be more inquisitive and take more risks. Yet, in follow-up calls, these managers complained that my clients question everything and seek my counsel to get their people to stop pushing back so much.

This is like asking your fitness trainer how you can increase your upper body strength while never leaving the couch. This simply can't be done.

I'm sure you don't get up each day asking yourself what you can do to stifle your people today, and if you could find a way to stop this negative behavior, you would. Here are some ideas to get you started.

Change Your Outlook about Inquisitiveness

Rather than viewing too much curiosity as a waste of time, consider that someone who is asking a lot of questions is taking a deep interest in another's ideas and that they have value to add to the conversation. Sometimes, the mere gesture of asking a question causes people to pause, reflect, and shift direction, which ultimately leads to a better path. Those who demonstrate an interest in what others have to say generally work together more effectively, which is needed if a team is to be successful.

Consider Curiosity to Be One of the Main Levers of Innovation

Most would consider Henry Ford to have been quite innovative. His curiosity and determination led him to build a reliable and affordable car that the average American worker could afford—the Model T. Somewhere along the line, Ford stopped experimenting and remained completely focused on improving the Model T. At the same time, consumers were no longer happy with only one option. They wanted a greater variety in their cars, which Ford was unwilling to provide. As a result, competitors such as General Motors started offering different models, and they were able to capture the market share quickly. If Ford had been a bit more curious and asked people *why* they wanted more variety, his company may have been able to meet their needs and retain their market position.

The Henry Ford story is an excellent reminder of what can happen when we are so internally focused that we forget to ask questions. Many of us are a lot like Ford. When we first start a job, we tend to view puzzling situations (including conversations) as exciting challenges. This excitement seems to wane the longer we are in a position. We no longer see obstacles as thrilling challenges. Instead, we view them as obstacles that are slowing us down in our time-starved world. Here's some irony for you. People are under so much pressure to produce that they're left with little time to ask questions that could result in new efficiencies, better products and services, and stronger workplace relationships.

Model Curiosity

Like it or not, your employees are watching and learning from you. If they observe you shutting down a coworker, or if someone on your team is penalized for a risk they've taken that didn't exactly go as planned, they're going to crawl into their shell and remain there until it's safe to come out again. I get how frustrating it can be when some-thing doesn't go according to plan. However, rather than criticize your employee, why not practice inquisitiveness? Here's how you might want to handle this scenario. "It's unfortunate that the time and money invested in this project didn't yield the results we were seeking. What do you think went wrong? Tell me why you made the decisions you made and if you had to do it over again, what, if anything, you'd do differently? What did you learn from this experience?"

This conversation is a lot more productive than the one where you say, "Wow, you really screwed this up. What the hell happened?"

Here's something that I've learned over the years that may be help-ful to you. Asking one or two of the *right* questions is much more potent than shooting off an array of questions, with the hope that one will hit the target. A large part of my practice is executive coach-ing. Every engagement starts with a 360-degree assessment, where I gather feedback from the coachee's stakeholders. I could easily use an automated system that would ask people to respond to dozens of questions—but I don't. I choose a more intimate approach, even if that means this will take a considerable amount of time for me to do. I call each stakeholder and ask two questions.

1 What does this person do well?

2 What is getting in his or her way?

Yep, that's it. I keep it simple, and as a result, I'm able to uncover the critical information I need to help my clients. With this in mind, when approaching high-stakes conversations, consider what *critical* information you need to move the conversation forward. Consider what one or two questions will allow you to cut through the noise and get straight to the point. Here are a few of my favorite groupings of questions that, as a leader, I've used to steer difficult conversations in the direction I want them to go.

- How did we get here?/Where do we go from here?
- What's really going on here?/What do you need from me to help you move forward?
- Are you having fun at work?/What do you enjoy most or find most unsatisfying about your job?

Curiosity versus Judgment

There's a fine line between coming across as curious and sounding judgmental. How you come across is all in the delivery, which is why it's essential to monitor your tone. You'll most likely appear to be judgmental if you ask a question like, "Why did you say that to him?" or "Why did you do it this way?" in a sharp tone. This will undoubtedly leave the other person with the impression that you are questioning their judgment rather than trying to gain a better understanding of what occurred.

Judgment is based on personal opinions and has its place, such as when you're asked to judge an office contest where employees are incentivized to come up with the best cost savings idea. However, unsolicited judgmental communication can be quite harmful when it is used in the workplace, especially if people are working on creative endeavors. It can quickly put people on the defense and stifle innovation for fear of being judged harshly. I've personally experienced what it's like to work for someone who came across as overly judgmental. As a result, I did exactly what was asked and nothing more, for fear that I would face her wrath. As soon as I realized this was her normal behavior, I put my resume in order and soon left the firm.

Judgmental people, rather than being curious, tend to look at everything through their own lens. Sound familiar? When you set certain expectations for yourself, and you evaluate everyone against your behavior, there's a good chance you'll come across as judgmental. For example, let's suppose an employee has made a mistake that resulted in the profit and loss statement being incorrect. You have a knack for finance, which seems to come naturally to you. However, finance is not your employee's strong suit. You sit down and have a discussion with this person to address this error. You may unconsciously be thinking, "This guy is not that smart." You then blurt out something like, "I don't get it. Numbers don't lie. Can't you see this?" Not only does the employee feel awful about the mistake, he feels terrible about himself, which gets you nowhere because he immediately shuts down.

Try to identify your triggers. Perhaps it's a specific topic, action, or a word that someone uses that brings you into the judgmental zone. I know I tend to go to judgment land when someone says to me, "I'll do it later," as I have little tolerance (okay, no tolerance) for people who procrastinate. I'm continually having to remind myself to take a breath before responding. When I pause, I often realize that what I'm about to say will not move the conversation where I want it to go. I'm mindful of my tone, and rather than respond, I choose to wait and see if "later" does come before pushing the matter any further.

Earlier, I mentioned the role nonverbal communication plays in terms of difficult workplace conversations. Even if we don't say a word, we can appear judgmental. We may unconsciously roll our eyes in response to something someone says or point our finger when we're speaking, a habit one of my employees had until I brought this matter to her attention. I was her boss, and she had an adult child my age. Whenever I'd say something she didn't like, she'd wag her finger at me and speak in a motherly voice, "Now Roberta..." This behavior always triggered me to lash back with a snide response. Finally, one day I decided to confront her about this behavior. When I did, she was stunned and said, "I had no idea I was wagging my finger at you when speaking." Her daughter later said she did this to her all the time. My employee apologized, and eventually, we got to a place where we could laugh about this. Of course, it's difficult to observe our nonverbal communication for ourselves. That's why I recommend you ask a trusted colleague to keep an eye out and to make you aware when you do something that dilutes or changes the message you're trying to send.

Here's a final tip to help ensure you appear curious rather than judgmental. Instead of using words like, "that's wrong" or "that's bad," consider saying, "that's interesting" or "tell me more," and then follow up with your observation. Remember, when you use nonjudgmental language, people are more apt to engage in conversation with you, which is precisely what we're seeking here.

The Impact Curiosity Has on Conversations

Have you ever had one of those one-sided conversations with someone? You know the kind where you start the conversation off with "How are you?" They reply with "Fine." You then ask, "What's up?" They respond with one word—"Nothing." It's even worse when you are in the midst of a difficult conversation and the other person gives you one word answers. You ask, "What's wrong?" and they reply, "Nothing." You *know* something is wrong, as their body language says it all. So, you say, "What do you mean nothing is wrong? It certainly feels like something is wrong." Eventually you get tired of talking to yourself, and as you walk away, you shake your head and say, "Whatever." In times like these, you want to be especially careful in terms of your tone and your choice of words. Think about what you might say and ask that will demonstrate to the other person your concern is authentic.

Using Curiosity to Your Advantage

Curiosity allows us to think more deeply and explore options that we may not have seen had we accepted what was in front of us, without question. Here's how a leader's inquisitiveness led to an outcome neither he nor his employee anticipated.

I had to counsel an employee, whom I inherited from my predecessor. On paper, he appeared to have the skills needed to do the job. However, he was struggling in a role that should have been a slam dunk for him. Things quickly went from terrible to worse. That's when I knew I had to speak with him. Our conversation began with, "Your contribution at last week's meeting has me worried. The agenda you put together was weak, and you barely spoke, even though you were the person who called the meeting. You can see why I'm alarmed, can't you?" He responded by saying, "I don't understand. You told me to let the subject matter experts speak, which is what I did." I then said, "Yes, I did say to be sure they had a chance to speak. However, after they finished, I expected you to comment as well. Your previous boss told me you were quite vocal in meetings. Were you not prepared for the meeting? Is that why you chose not to comment? Did you not receive the weekly flash report in time? Is there something else going on that I should know about?"

After a moment of silence, he said, "I feel like an administrative assistant. All I do is put together meetings and send out the recap of what's transpired." I responded by saying, "Our department wouldn't function without your organizational skills. Was the job not fully explained to you by my predecessor before you accepted this role? Assuming that you're able to improve your performance and carry on your current tasks, what else would you like to be doing?"

It's been six months since our initial conversation. We had several follow-up meetings, and eventually, the employee and I agreed that he was better suited for a different role in the organization. If I had assumed that I had inherited someone else's problem, it would have been just a matter of time before I fired him. My sense of curiosity led me to ask probing questions that allowed us to reach a mutually agreed upon solution. From what I hear, he's blossoming in his new role.

Anonymous

All too often, when counseling employees, we default to the "this person has got to go" position. This case study demonstrates how a more favorable outcome (for all involved) is possible when you're open to understanding why people behave in a particular way. This sense of curiosity will serve you well, especially as you assume additional responsibilities and manage more people in the organization.

Determining the best way to open a difficult conversation seems to be challenging for many, which is why it's worth taking a deeper dive into this topic. How you start the conversation can determine the outcome, so it's essential to give this consideration. Here's where curiosity can be an asset. Although the book is titled *Can We Talk?*, I'd advise against starting any challenging work conversation with this question, as doing so will immediately put the person on the defense. Thoughts like, "Oh no, what did I do?" or "Oh boy, now what?" will no doubt be circulating in someone's head when they hear these words. When this occurs, the other party will immediately begin thinking about how to defend themselves best and hear little of what you have to say.

Starting difficult conversations is tough. I was coaching the CEO of a tech company who happen to be conflict avoidant. For months, I advised him to fire his second in command, who seemed to be sucking the air out of the organization. The majority of our conversations were about this executive's performance or, in this case, lack of performance. Finally, I asked my client what was holding him back from telling this employee exactly how he felt. He said he didn't know how to start this conversation. At that moment, I realized that discomfort around starting courageous conversations isn't limited to rank-and-file managers—CEOs and senior leaders are also very much in need of guidance on this issue.

With this in mind, here are some curious conversation starters. Feel free to adapt the language to reflect better your personality and the seriousness of the conversation at hand:

- I need your help with something. Do you have a moment to discuss this with me?

- I'd like to understand your feelings about __ better and share my perspective as well.

- Something has been on my mind lately that I'd like to discuss with you. I'm hoping you can provide me with some insights so I can better understand.

- I think we have different ideas on how to approach this project. I'd like to hear your thinking on this and then share mine.

- You're probably as surprised as I am in terms of what just happened. Got a minute to talk?

- I have something that I'd like to talk with you about that I believe will allow us to work more effectively together. Can we schedule a time to meet this week or next?

- I'm wondering if you can share your thinking regarding a particular situation, so I can better understand your response.

- I'm curious. Can you tell me why you chose to go in this direction?

- I'm not going to beat around the bush here. I think we both have things we'd like to say to one another. Would you like to start, or should I?

Now that you've got the most challenging part behind you (opening the conversation), you're ready to tackle the challenge of keeping the conversation from quickly closing. If you think about it, closed-ended questions can make the person on the other end of the table feel like they're being interrogated, which is an approach that is best avoided if you want to keep the conversation going, unless of course you genuinely are interrogating someone. To keep the other person actively engaged, I recommend using open-ended questions which, unlike closed-ended questions, typically can't be answered using a single word. Open-ended questions will allow you to solicit the other person's thoughts, feelings, ideas, and suggestions, allowing you to have a more in-depth and richer conversation.

You may find yourself in a conversation that's about to end abruptly and without the resolution you had hoped for. Should this happen, it's time to turn up the curiosity and ask open-ended questions. A genuine curiosity will help you create open-ended questions that are meaningful and help you achieve your goal or allow you to gather the data you are seeking. When formulating your questions, think about what information you'd really like to know from your respondent. It's also important to remember that it's highly likely that an open-ended question will lead to tangential offshoots, which is a good thing because it means your open-ended questions got the other person thinking. Be open (no pun intended) to other issues that may arise that may need your attention.

Here are some examples of open-ended questions that will show the other person you're interested in gaining a better understanding, which will keep the conversation flowing:

- What else can you tell me about X?
- What did you use as the basis of your decision?
- What exactly happened that caused you to react this way?
- Why don't you explain your side of the story?
- How are you feeling about X?
- What challenges do you see for you to achieve your objectives?
- How do you suggest we measure success?
- How do you see this playing out?
- Where do we go from here?
- If we were to meet six months from now, what needs to happen for you to feel like we've worked through this issue?

Regaining Control When a Conversation Derails

Sometimes, regardless of how prepared you are for a challenging conversation, your discussion derails. Earlier in the book, I mentioned Lila, the most challenging employee I've ever managed. Lila probably should have been a magician, as she was a master in misdirection. We'd be discussing an issue like her constant tardiness, and she'd say things like, "Lots of people come into work late" or "It seems to me that you're singling me out." Naturally, these responses were not ones I had anticipated. Admittedly, there were many times when Lila was successful in shifting the conversation away from her and toward someone else. As I noted, I was a young manager, and Lila was a force to be reckoned with. I now have considerable experience managing the Lilas of the world and am better equipped to advise my clients on managing through these conversations. Here are some suggestions to help you regain control of a conversation that has gone off track.

Take Responsibility

As I mentioned in the introduction, it takes two people to have a productive conversation. Often conversations go off track because we're not direct enough. To spare someone's feelings, we may say something like, "You're a great employee. However, I have to let you go as your performance is no longer up to par." Can you see why an employee would be confused by this statement and might respond with, "Why are you letting me go? You, yourself, said I was a great employee!"?

The way to regain control in a situation like this one is to reset the conversation by saying, "I can see why this might be confusing. Perhaps, I'm not explaining myself clearly. Over the past six months, we've had extensive meetings regarding missed deadlines, careless mistakes, and your lack of interest in working as a productive member of this team. At our last meeting, I said that if you weren't able to turn this situation around, you would no longer be employed with the company. I'm sorry to say that today is your last day of employment. Your final check is in the envelope, along with information regarding the continuation of your healthcare benefits."

Seek Input to Problem-Solve

You're not going to get far in terms of coming up with a workable solution if the other party feels like they're being told they're the reason there's a problem in the first place. Think about a time when you may have felt threatened. Perhaps you were on the other side of the conversation and felt like your boss was blaming the entire team's failure on you. Here's where a simple and effective approach called "feedforward," a term crafted by executive coach Marshall Goldsmith, and a practice that I learned when I became certified in Marshall's Stakeholder Centered Coaching, can be extremely handy.

Instead of focusing on the past, elicit advice on what people can do to get better in the future. For example, suppose you're counseling a manager who appears to be having difficulty trusting employees to get their work done correctly. Most leaders would say something like, "Susan, you've got to stop micromanaging your people." Confused, Susan would probably respond by saying, "Okay." Or if she feels you're the one who is the micromanager, she may even say, "I'm glad you brought up this issue of micromanagement, as I've meant to speak to you about this."

Using the concept of feedforward, instead of focusing on the past, you would ask, "What are one or two things you think you could do that will help you gain more productivity both personally and on behalf of your team?" Now, here's where the challenging part comes in. When the person responds, don't try to correct them. Say, "Great!" If they've missed the mark, keep asking, "What else can you do?" until they're in the ballpark. Feedforward is an excellent reminder that no one wants to relive the past over and over again and that doing so usually results in people blaming one another rather than coming up with viable ideas that can be put into action. The practice of feedforward is also a great way to encourage employees to look to the future and continue to move forward.

Keep the Focus Where It Needs to Be

If I had a dime for every time an employee I was counseling brought another employee's name into the conversation, I would have been able to retire years ago! You've probably heard or may even have said things like, "Bob is always taking extra time at lunch as well. Will you also be speaking with Bob?" or "If I had received approval for more headcount as Denise got, I'm sure we wouldn't be having this chat." Bob, Denise, Sam, John... I've heard it all, and here's what I always say: "We're not talking about X. We're here to discuss you." I'm not going to lie to you and say that from this point forward, the focus is entirely on the employee, as many employees will not accept this as your final answer, meaning you may need to repeat this statement more than once.

Sometimes you'll be asked specifically about a particular person who is also known to be struggling. I coach my clients to respond with, "I'm sure you can appreciate that my conversations with this other person are confidential, just like my conversations with you are strictly between us." Not even Lila can argue with a statement like this! I then advise my clients to move the conversation back to the matter at hand.

The next chapter is on compromise. Most difficult conversations will involve some give and take, which can be challenging for some. It's not always clear if you should plow full steam ahead or take a step back so you can move things forward. We'll explore this and more in chapter 5.

KEY LEARNING POINTS

- Being curious and asking questions to learn more about a particular situation shows the other party that you're interested in what they have to say, which helps to move a conversation forward.

- Minding your own business might be great advice in some circumstances. However, there are certainly times when the need to be curious supersedes the worry associated with being considered a busybody.

- Although most leaders would like to believe they value inquisitive minds, in reality, most stifle curiosity. You can become more inquisitive by changing your outlook, meaning viewing curiosity as a way to add value, rather than as a time waster.

- Like it or not, your employees are watching and learning from you. If they observe you shutting down a coworker, or if someone on your team is penalized for a risk they've taken that didn't exactly go as planned, they're going to crawl into their shell and remain there until it's safe to come out again.

- Asking one or two of the *right* questions is much more potent than shooting off an array of questions, with the hope that one will hit the target.

- There's a fine line between coming across as curious and sounding judgmental. How you come across is all in the delivery, which is why it's essential to monitor your tone.

- Discomfort around starting courageous conversations isn't limited to rank-and-file managers—CEOs and senior leaders are also very much in need of guidance on this issue.

- When you find yourself in a conversation that's about to end abruptly, and without the resolutions you had hoped for, turn up the curiosity and ask open-ended questions to help move the conversation forward.

- When formulating your questions, think about what information you'd really like to know from your respondent. It's also important to remember that it's highly likely that an open-ended question will lead to tangential offshoots, which is a good thing because it means your open-ended questions got the other person thinking.

- Sometimes, regardless of how prepared you are for a challenging conversation, your discussion derails. You can get back on track by taking responsibility for any missteps, seeking input to problem-solve, and keeping the focus where it needs to be.

05

Compromise

Earn Respect by Respecting Others

Compromise is an agreement or a resolution of a dispute that is reached by each side making concessions. That sounds like a fairly reasonable idea. Yet, getting to a place where both parties feel good about a resolution is harder than it looks. The same can be said about speaking with someone about a challenging topic, which is why I've included compromise as one of the seven principles of navigating difficult conversations at work. In this chapter, we'll explore how to achieve mutual respect and find common ground. I'll show you how to work through a conversation so that each party feels whole at the end of the discussion. We'll spend considerable time discussing the topic of using influence, as this is a skill that can help you both personally and professionally. We'll look at when and how to agree to disagree, as well as how taking a step back can help move you forward. We'll end the chapter with some signs to be on the lookout for that may indicate you're about to hit a dead end.

Achieving Mutual Respect

Several years ago, I worked with a senior-level executive at a financial services firm, who grew up in an era where the only way to win was for the other guy to lose. This attitude permeated his industry, which was considered to be very cutthroat. He confided in me that he thought every organization operated this way, as this was all he knew.

Recently, he reached out to me, asking for help. About a year ago, he took early retirement from the firm and accepted a position with a nonprofit where he had previously volunteered. He told me that he struggled to navigate a work environment based on collaboration rather than alienation. I assured him that this was an area I was well equipped to help him with.

You may find comfort in knowing that you're not the only person navigating an environment that is entirely different than the one that you came from. Lots of people have grown up in organizations where there can only be one winner. However, times have changed (okay, there are certainly some companies still living in the dark ages), and organizations appear to be shifting to a more collaborative work culture. To survive and thrive in this new environment, you must embrace the idea of compromise.

Unhealthy competition is about winning at all costs and is a losing strategy for resolving conflict. In comparison, compromise is a give-and-take proposition. We each get a little of what we want. People who have mutual respect for one another are more likely to compromise than those who don't. For example, let's say you're having a heated discussion with a coworker whom you don't respect. Your approach to designing a new product requires a different methodology than what he's suggesting. You quickly dismiss his approach as terrible. You refuse even to consider the possibility that some of what he's proposing has any virtue. Your conversation lasts about a minute and ends with each party returning to their corner of the boxing ring with no resolution in sight.

Now think about an intense discussion you may have had with a coworker whom you respect. Your teammate listens to your suggestion and acknowledges that there is merit in what you're recommending. She then says, "You know, Ron, that's an interesting way to approach this project. You raise some great points. What if we took this one step further and involved the marketing team while we are still in the product development stage?" You have a lot of respect for this colleague, and she feels the same way about you. While you may not be in complete agreement regarding bringing in the marketing team just yet, you respond to her with a counterproposal. You say, "Hmm, I hadn't thought of bringing in the marketing team this early in the process. It's an interesting idea. However, I'm a bit concerned we may not be quite ready for them. What if we were to wait just a bit and bring them in after we've completed the prototype? This way, they'd have a better sense of the features and benefits of our product, and we'd still have time to make changes to the prototype, should they suggest ideas that we think are worth implementing." Your colleague agrees to your proposed timeline. In this scenario, both parties seem open to hearing what the other person has to say and are willing to give a bit regarding how the project should be run. We call this a compromise. In all likelihood, the end product will be far better than what was originally proposed, and both parties will feel good about their contribution.

The next time you find yourself in a high-stakes situation or in a conversation with someone you don't particularly like, think of the late, great superstar Aretha Franklin. Aretha made the word "respect" famous when she sang about it in the summer of 1967, and it still rings true. Respect is something we all yearn for, and at times, it feels like it's in short supply in the workplace.

Recognizing that difficult conversations may be more challenging for some people than others is the first step toward establishing a respectful relationship with someone who may not see things the way you do. Start by setting your differences aside (at least for the moment) and approach all conversations with the mindset that you will not pass judgment on what the other person has to say until they've finished completing their thought. Before replying to what someone has said, take a moment to think about your response. Then ask yourself, "Is there anything they've said that I can build upon?" followed by "What is the minimum and maximum that I'd like to get out of this conversation?" Building on what someone else says, in a positive way, demonstrates to the other party that you're truly listening. The second question regarding your minimum and maximum will help you clarify what you're willing to give up to get to a place of agreement. Here's an example of how this might play out.

Let's say you're going to ask your boss for a raise, which everyone finds hard to do. Your boss has a reputation for being pretty tight with the budget. You know this from personal experience, as you're still fuming from when she gave you an outstanding review and a paltry raise. It was at that moment in time that you lost all respect for her.

Your boss tells you that she can increase your salary, but not by much. You slam your hand on the table and respond by saying, "What's it going to take for me to be paid fairly? You keep telling me that my performance is good. Yet, I keep getting paltry raises." You can see from your boss's face that she's less than pleased with your outburst. Yet, you go on. "I'm going to find a job where I'm paid what I'm worth." You regret these words as soon as they come out of your mouth. Jobs in your field are challenging to find these days, and without even knowing it, you've just put your boss on notice that you're exiting. Your boss says, "I'll assume from this conversation that you're giving me your two-week notice. We'll miss having you around here."

You set the conversation up with no room for compromise. You backed your boss into a corner and made threats, which resulted in a reaction you hadn't anticipated. You're officially on the job market!

As hard as it might be, you need to push these feelings of mistrust to the side—at least for now. The outstanding review with a small raise happened several years ago when the company was going through a difficult time financially. Here's how the conversation could have gone had you set the stage for a dialogue rather than an altercation.

Before addressing your boss, ask yourself what you'd ideally like in terms of a raise and, if need be, what you will settle for. If you know this going into the conversation, you'll be more apt to compromise, which could work in your favor. Here's how. You sit down with your boss to review your contribution to the firm. You've had a terrific year, and your boss acknowledges this. She then tells you that, unfortunately, she wasn't able to get you the whole amount you had asked for. She could only get a 3 percent raise approved, which is slightly below your minimum. You're disappointed. You say to your boss, "You know, I was hoping to receive at least a 4 percent raise." She agrees that you deserve more and says, "Yes, I was disappointed as well. How about if we work together to get you ready for a promotion. I can probably make that happen by year-end. The promotion will come with a pay increase that will surpass what you're hoping for. Does that sound like a fair compromise?" You enthusiastically say, "Sure!" Had you approached this conversation with a lack of respect for your boss, your response might have been to try and win a losing battle. Your emotions would have taken over, and there's a reasonably good chance you would have said things that you'd later regret, which is what happened in the first scenario. In the end, it appears that your willingness to compromise will get you way more than your stated maximum.

When two people mutually respect each other, they'll continue the dialogue. The moment either party perceives disrespect, the conversation is no longer about the original topic. The offended party (or parties) will immediately go into defensive mode to preserve their dignity—usually at all costs. I can recall this happening with a peer, whom we'll call Jeff. Admittedly, Jeff wasn't my favorite person to be around. He was one of these people who came across as someone who felt superior to others—I'm sure you've met his kind. As director of human resources, I was responsible for signing off on all salary increases and was instructed by my boss, the vice president, to "kick-back" any raises that were higher than what was budgeted for.

It was annual review time, and Jeff came to me fully expecting me to approve his pay increases for his department, even though several proposed increases were over budget. Our conversation started civilly. Being a highly strategic person, Jeff waited until after I had approved most of the pay increases to present me with several that were way out of line. The conversation went like this.

Me: Jeff, I'm unable to approve these salary increases. They're higher than what's in the merit budget.

Jeff: You don't understand. Without these people, there would be no company.

Me: I understand this must be frustrating for you. However, if I make an exception, others will expect exceptions as well.

The conversation remained cordial until Jeff said, "Listen, you just don't get it, do you?" That one statement changed the intent of our discussion. In a matter of seconds, we went from talking about salary increases to me defending my dignity. Had Jeff taken a more respectful tone with me, I may have politely suggested that he take this up directly with our boss.

If I could have this conversation again, I would do things differently. The moment Jeff slung that line at me, I would have taken a step back and taken a deep breath. Although, at times, Jeff certainly could be obnoxious, I doubt he intentionally meant to call my judgment into question. I would have looked for a mutually agreeable solution—a compromise of some sort. I would have let go of the idea that my hands were tied and would have said, "It feels like we both have a strong opinion on this. Let's take a step back here and see if we can find a solution that satisfies both of us." In all likelihood, Jeff might have asked, "What do you have in mind?" or he would have presented an alternative solution to the matter at hand. If both of us hadn't been so headstrong, we could have figured something out.

Of course, it's much easier to think and act clearly and professionally when you're on the outside of a highly charged conversation looking in. With considerable practice, you'll learn how to keep your emotions in check, improve your ability to read people, and be more open to finding an acceptable solution. Aim for progress—not perfection.

Finding Common Ground

Some days, it feels like the only thing we can agree on is that we can't agree. Here's the thing. Disagreement isn't necessarily a bad thing—that is, if we can disagree productively. Disagreement usually comes down to one thing—perspective. This may help to explain why people have completely opposite opinions about a particular political candidate. Those who can't find a way to have a courteous discussion are the people who are unable or unwilling to see things through some-one else's eyes.

Over the past few years, I have seen friendships crack by differing points of view. I have watched, observed, and participated in conversations that broke down in the middle of negotiations because one or both parties refused to consider the other person's point of view. These kinds of conversations have turned into some pretty unpleasant altercations.

Here are a few suggestions to help reduce the discord and create an environment where progress can be made without permanent damage to the relationships of those involved.

Focus on the Why

Why have you decided to meet? Why have you chosen to discuss a particular topic? Why is it vital that you come to an understanding? When everyone understands why something needs to be achieved, there is a foundation to find common ground. For example, I have a client who recently approached me to coach one of her employees. When she first introduced the idea of coaching, her employee immediately became defensive. It wasn't until she focused on the why that she was able to get her employee to see that they were both working toward a common goal—getting this employee to a place where she was respected by her peers. My client made some allowances regarding the timing of when the coaching would begin and agreed to her employee's request to choose her coach. In the end, she selected me.

Keep Your Eyes on the Prize

When in meetings or a thorny conversation, it's easy to go off course. You may feel a certain way is the best course of action, while a colleague thinks his way is best. Keep the reason for your meeting top of mind. If you find you're getting frustrated, remind yourself of what you're trying to accomplish. Don't try to win every battle. You won't. Instead, focus on the big picture. Give yourself *permission* to find common ground.

Be Open to All Alternatives

Have you ever found yourself arguing with someone only to discover that you were both saying the same thing? I have. These conversations usually end with someone stating, "Hey, what are we fighting about? We're saying the same thing!" If you're open to finding results and not set on getting the other person to agree with your approach, you'll be able to find common ground. Generally speaking, there is usually more than one way to solve a problem.

Try to Understand the Other Person's Perspective

Work on being less argumentative. When someone expresses an opinion that you don't necessarily agree with, say, "Thank you for sharing your thoughts." There's no need to respond to everything the other person says. Instead, focus on listening. By doing so, you're more likely to hear cues that indicate you've reached common ground.

If you continue to have trouble finding common ground, you may need to bring in a third party to help you work through the situation. An objective third party can help you defuse tension, explain your points more clearly, and identify areas of mutual understanding.

You Cut, I'll Choose

Like most parents, I struggled with how to divide things evenly among my two children, who are close in age. I remember many intense arguments over silly things like who was entitled to the bigger slice of cake (although they looked to be the same size to me). The topic of how to ensure neither child felt slighted was one that I frequently discussed with other parents. Coming up with a workable solution seemed like an impossible task—that is until a child psychologist suggested that I let the kids work it out. Desperate to end the tension, I asked her how to do this when you're dealing with a seven- and eight-year-old. She said, "That's easy. Have one kid cut a slice of cake or whatever you're trying to split, and then the other gets to choose which slice they'd prefer." Eureka! Best parenting and work life advice ever! Let me explain.

For a relationship to prosper, both parties must get something out of it. Each party must feel like they're being treated fairly. When approaching tough conversations, consider what's being proposing versus what you're expecting. Is what's being asked of you or the other party relatively fair and reasonable? Can you be a bit more generous in terms of the "slice" you're offering? Can you both come away from this situation feeling like you've each gotten some of what you need? Let's say someone from another team makes a request from your team, and it appears more than what you can reasonably do. Your first instinct may be to say no. This response could come back to haunt you. Your coworker might then go to your manager, which would not bode well for you. Or, if in the future you needed the help of your coworker's team, he might return the favor by saying no. What if instead, you looked for a way to come up with a workable solution? What if you said you could take on the task, but that your colleague would need to be flexible in terms of the deadline? What, if anything, about this person's request is unreasonable? Explain your logic, so that your coworker trusts you've given the request ample consideration. Then ask this person if they can see another way for your team to get this done.

In work and in life, we're not always going to get *everything* we want. However, it's nice to know that someone has made an effort to meet us in the middle. And when they do, this is something we rarely forget.

An executive shared a story with me on how, by figuring out how she could meet the other person's needs, along with her own, they both could come out winners. Here's her story:

I was hired for a new customer service manager role and was enjoying my job. Things seemed to be going well—until the company changed hands, and I was assigned a new boss. I was nervous that my job would potentially be on the chopping block, as my requests for previously promised staff were denied and meetings with my new manager suddenly became less frequent.

After a few sleepless nights, I decided to address this situation with my boss. I composed an email telling him how I was feeling and asked him if we could talk. I started our conversation off by explaining why I was feeling unsettled. Here's what I said: "Before our company was acquired, I was hired into the newly created position of customer service manager by your predecessor. I was assured this was a key role and that I would be given the resources needed to get my department up and running." I then went on to say, "Since the company changed hands, most of my requests for resources have been denied." My boss responded by saying, "Let me be honest with you. We already have someone who is doing some of the job functions you've been assigned. We're trying to figure out if we have some redundancies here and how to handle things best. We aren't going to approve any expenditures for your area until we sort this out."

I knew that I was feeling especially vulnerable, as I had left a good-paying job for this opportunity, so I took a moment to compose myself and thought about what a good compromise might look like. I then said, "Look, I get that the job that I was hired for may not be the job that I'm in after the integration is complete. If I need to, I'm willing to work under this other person." I could tell my boss was relieved. He responded by saying, "I appreciate your flexibility. It may not come to that. However, would you be open to considering a new role? We've been discussing the importance of the customer experience and may be looking for someone to lead this initiative. You won't have day-to-day interactions with customers. However, you'll still be involved in customer care. Is this something you'd be interested in exploring?"

Several months later, I was reassigned and am now the lead person in charge of the customer experience. This role is a better fit for me, and I'm happier than I've ever been.

Anonymous

This person could have quickly gone on the defense when her boss told her that her job was at risk. Instead, she took a step back and thought about what she might be willing to settle for. Her boss appreciated that she made this conversation more comfortable for him and rewarded her with an even better position than the one she was hired for. She respectfully approached her boss and stayed composed throughout the conversation, which helped her think more clearly. This is a lesson we can all benefit from. Staying calm and seeking a middle ground provides both parties with an opportunity to come up with alternatives that neither party may have considered before entering into the conversation.

I, too, have used compromise quite successfully. Earlier in my career, I was let go from a job that I didn't particularly like. In those days, you stood a much better chance of finding a new job when you were gainfully employed than when you were not. One day, my boss called me in to tell me he was letting me go. I sort of knew this was coming, which allowed me to think about what I wanted to ask for on my way out the door. I knew that my responsibilities would fall on his shoulders, so I proposed the following. I said, "I agree that this job isn't a good fit for me. What if you allowed me to stay on while I look for a new job? I can keep everything going for you while you look to hire my replacement." I could see from the look on his face that he was relieved. You see, the company was in the middle of a big corporate move, which he was responsible for. Having one less thing to deal with during this extremely stressful time was more than appealing to him. He also wouldn't have to explain to people why I was no longer with the company. He could say that the commute to the new offices was more than I was willing to do. It was a win-win situation all around. I stayed on and launched my consulting practice, and I was able to train my replacement, which meant considerably less work for him. No matter which side of the conversation you're on, always look to see if there is a way for both parties to compromise and come out as winners. You'll both be glad you did.

You Want Me to Do What?
Using Influence To Get What You Need

You probably know people who seem to have been born with what I call the influencing gene. They appear to have a natural ability to convince people to go along with whatever they suggest. As of this writing, there is no scientific evidence that the ability to influence is actually part of our DNA. Luckily for most of us, influencing is a skill that we can learn.

I define influence as asking for something you need in a way that allows the other person to say yes to whatever you've presented, which is exactly what want we want someone to do when we're in the middle of a challenging conversation. Throughout this book, I've been discussing the connection between healthy relationships and productive discussions. If you have a trusting relationship with someone, it will be that much easier to convince them to do what you'd like them to do. Without that relationship, the other person may view you as being manipulative. For example, let's say you're speaking to a manager, and you want to move her to another position. You're unsure how she'll react to this news. If you have a stable relationship with this person, she'll most likely believe you have her best interests in mind. If you don't, she may think you have an ulterior motive, such as wanting to move her out so you can give this position to someone she thinks you favor.

Here are some techniques to help you become better at influencing.

Make Daily Deposits into Your Bank of Trust Account

Earlier in this book, I introduced the bank of trust model. Since the chances of influencing someone who doesn't trust you during a heated conversation are about the same as experiencing snow in Hawaii, you can see why this bears repeating. Do something every day to build trust. This could be as simple as doing what you say you'll do.

Check Your Relationship Status

Every relationship has its ups and downs. The condition your relationship is in on the day you're attempting to bring someone to your side of the conversation is what matters most. Let's say you and your colleague had a difference of opinion earlier this week. You're not especially proud of how you handled yourself, as you said some things you immediately regretted. I wouldn't advise you to seek a compromise on another matter until you've repaired the relationship.

Make Sure Your Request Is Specific

Have you ever had someone try to influence you to do something, only you weren't quite sure what they were asking? You may have felt like they were trying to confuse you intentionally. You may have even walked away, feeling manipulated. When using influence, it's always best to tell the person precisely what you'd like them to do. This sets the stage for an honest conversation and allows you the option of modifying your request based on this person's reaction. Here's an example of a specific influencing request, which I use when training leaders to be more influential. Suppose you're in a heated discussion with an employee. Rather than saying, "I need you to pull your weight around here," instead, say, "I need you to perform better in your job. By that, I mean, create the project strategy, assign tasks to the team, and follow-up with your coworkers weekly." The second statement clearly explains your expectations and moves the conversation forward in a productive way.

Think W.I.F.M. (What's in It for Me)

Earlier, I talked about the need to put yourself in someone else's place. Master influencers do this all the time. They ask themselves why someone would consider their request—W.I.F.M.—then make that reason part of that request. Building upon the example I presented for making your request specific, the conversation would go like this: "I need you to perform better in your job. By that, I mean, create the project strategy, assign tasks to the team, and follow-up with your coworkers weekly. By doing so, you'll be freed up to work with me on the selection of the new computer software you've been advocating for."

Let's put this together. You'd like an employee to shift over to a new account. However, you're concerned he may not want to give up his most lucrative account. You have high levels of trust and a strong relationship with this person. You're in an excellent position to make an influencing request. Let's give it a go: "Sam, we've worked with one another for quite some time, and I've always encouraged you to learn different sides of the business. I'd like you to consider making a lateral move to a new account. By that I mean, you'll use the skills you've mastered on this account and become the lead person on the new account. This way you'll have the full-cycle agency experience, which in turn will best position you to head up the department."

Suppose you skipped any of the steps outlined above and simply told Sam you were taking away his most lucrative account (which you have the right to do because you're the boss) without further explanation. In that case, the conversation could have gotten argumentative. Sam would have told you all the reasons why this was a terrible idea, and you most likely would have pushed back until you reached a point where you might have said, "I'm in charge here, and that's my decision." There would have been no room for compromise, and Sam may have decided, right then and there, to look for a new job.

Learning how to move people to your way of thinking takes practice and requires the willingness to give up a small slice of what you may want right now to get to a place where both parties feel satisfied with what they've received.

Stepping Back to Move Forward

When you think about a difficult conversation, it's good to remember that the best path forward might involve a step back. This is not unlike the airline announcement we've all heard many times before takeoff: "Keep in mind that the closest exit may be behind you." It may be challenging to wrap your head around the idea that you can move a difficult conversation forward by taking a step back. That's because we're accustomed to thinking that backward moves equate to failure, or at least losing ground.

Often, when we take a step back, we're able to take an even more significant leap forward than would be impossible had we not done so. By stepping back, we can create the space needed to envision a new pathway we can take together.

I recall an uncomfortable situation that I needed to address with my boss. I felt like she was treating me differently (and not in a good way) than my peers. This feeling led to a conversation that went like this: "It feels to me that you're a lot tougher on me than you are with my peers. Whenever I suggest something in a meeting, you quickly dismiss what I'm saying. When others make similar remarks, you acknowledge their contribution and ask them to elaborate."

She responded by saying, "You know, you're right. I do this because you have the ability to think more deeply than most. Yet, the ideas you present are fairly basic. I expect more from you and am trying to get you to be bolder in your thinking."

She then did something I never thought she'd do. She apologized—her willingness to admit that her approach had been wrong allowed me to step back and probe further. I responded by saying, "Your apology means a lot to me. Thank you. Can we spend the next few minutes going over some examples of how I could have presented more fully developed ideas, and can we discuss this further in our weekly meetings?" She agreed. We spent the next six months having some incredibly rich conversations, and when I presented fully fleshed out ideas in meetings, she acknowledged me for my contribution. A year later, I received a promotion that a number of my colleagues had applied for.

I entered into our initial conversation with the goal of getting my boss to acknowledge my contributions every now and again. Instead, I came out with her willingness to coach me, which eventually led to a promotion that sent my career in a new and exciting direction. This would never have happened if I hadn't stepped back to move forward.

There are many times when it makes sense to take a step back. Here are a few:

- When your current approach isn't working.
- If you're feeling stuck, it's essential to take a break and reassess where you're headed.
- When the conversation feels more challenging than it should.

- When a discussion gets so heated up that it feels like things are about to explode.
- When you're trying hard to move the conversation forward, and the other party isn't responding.
- When you've lost sight of the real reason why you wanted to have the conversation in the first place.
- When you find that you're losing confidence, sometimes pausing and hitting the reset button can get you back on track.

Remember, taking a step back is not a sign of failure. It's a sign of maturity. What usually follows is a period of growth and improvement.

Dialing Down Highly Charged Conversations

I love my brother Mark dearly; however, whenever the topic of politics comes up, we wind up in a highly charged situation—well, more like a screaming match, where he raises his voice and I then raise mine. The conversation usually ends with me calmly saying, "I'm done." If you can believe this, our conversations used to be even more animated, which caused my blood pressure to rise to levels that were alarming! Over the years, I've learned how to dial down the volume, and at times have even had a civil conversation with him on the topic of politics.

Many of the uncomfortable situations that you will have to address at work run the risk of heating up, and may even boil over, especially if one or both parties are set on winning (whatever that means) or the discussion is around a subject that either party is passionate about.

Here's how to reset the thermostat when you need to take things down a notch.

Maintain Control of the Conversation

The moment the other party starts to deflect or tries to change the direction, pull the reins back and remind them again what you're seeking to achieve. When this occurs, try saying something like, "Danny, that's not the issue we're talking about. We're here to discuss…" Note: You may need to say this more than once.

Inquire and Validate

Sometimes the other person just wants to get something off their chest, and other times they are looking for you to take action. When you're unsure of what's needed of you, you'll need to ask. For example, you might say, "It sounds like this is very important to you. Are you wanting me to listen or are you asking for my opinion?" If they say they want your opinion, and your past experience with this person tells you that's not quite the case, consider asking, "What do you see as some possible solutions here?"

Don't Talk over One Another

Before jumping in, confirm with the other party that they are done presenting their case. Then begin your reply by saying, "Here's what I heard you say." By doing so, you'll demonstrate to the other party that you're actively listening, which will help to diffuse the situation. Should the other party start talking before you're finished, put up your hand and say, "I'm not done talking yet."

Eliminate the Word, "But" from Your Vocabulary

As soon as the word "but" comes out of your mouth, the other person will naturally go on the defense. From here, the conversation will quickly go downhill. Instead, respond to what the other person is saying with, "Yes, and." This will send a signal that you're open to building upon what was said, rather than appearing to be pushing your own agenda forward.

Avoid Accusatory Language

I've been on the receiving end of conversations where the other person insinuates that it's my fault that we're in the situation. When this happens, that doesn't make me want to work with them to come up with a solution. Nope. I just want to prove they are wrong. That's why I encourage my clients to start tough conversations by using the words, "I feel." No one can dispute your feelings. However, they can certainly tell you that you're mistaken when you make an accusatory statement like, "You're treating me unfairly."

State Your Appreciation for Their Willingness to Have the Conversation

No matter how the conversation goes with my brother, I always thank him for enlightening me. You should consider doing the same when someone is willing to discuss a sticky situation. Of course, if this person is your boss, you'll want to choose your words carefully, as thanking your supervisor for enlightening you may come across as a bit snarky. Instead, consider repeating back what they just said. "So, what I'm hearing you say is..." Followed by, "I appreciate your willingness to give me an opportunity to explain."

Agree to Take a Break

Sometimes, no matter how hard you try, you are unable to deescalate things. When this occurs, it's best to agree to take a break and to come back to the table when you've both had some time to cool off. By stepping back from a heated dialogue, you may begin to see things differently. Who knows, you may even wind up changing your position entirely, or you may at least get to a place where you can agree to disagree.

Caution: Dead End Ahead

Discussions about hard topics at work, such as employee performance, reductions-in-force, and disappointment with coworkers, can feel like playing with fire. These conversations have been lighting up workplaces for years. That's because the stakes are so high. Our reputation and livelihood are at risk, which causes us to go into defensive mode immediately when we feel threatened.

There will be situations where you'll reach a point where a compromise is no longer an option. With that in mind, here are some signs that you've reached the end of the road.

You Want More for Someone Than They Want for Themselves

It's taken me years to learn that you can't want more for someone than they want for themselves. Earlier, I told you the story of Lila, who tested me in more ways than I knew possible. She was a bright young lady with lots of potential, who I thought I could save. I about died trying. You see, I wanted more for Lila than she wanted for herself. I knew in my heart that I could help her get to a place where she'd blossom. The problem was that Lila was perfectly happy being a mediocre employee.

Here's my advice to you. If you're in the middle of an uncomfortable work conversation with someone, and it becomes evident to you that the other party isn't interested in coming to a compromise, give yourself permission to pause. Then ask, "Are you interested in us finding a way to move forward together, or should we stop here?" If the answer is no, stop there, then rest assured whatever you might have said would have fallen on deaf ears.

You're Overly Accommodating

Have you ever found yourself in a situation where, in an attempt to come across as flexible, you offered up more than you should have? The other person happily accepted whatever you proposed and offered nothing in return. The conversation ended, and you soon realized you'd given up way too much and the other person hadn't given up a thing.

Compromise is about *each* side making concessions. If you find you're the only one giving anything up, try this: "It feels like I'm the only one who is willing to give something up here for us to find a solution we can both live with. Where are you willing to bend, in terms of this situation?" If the other party isn't open to compromising, move on. People will take advantage of you—that is, if you let them.

You're Constantly Hoping the Other Party Will Change

Let's be honest. Like my peer Jeff, the difficult coworker who expected me to automatically approve pay raises for his department that were way over budget, some people simply don't buy into the concept of compromise. It's got to be their way or no way. I truly thought I could get Jeff to bend just a tad. In retrospect, I was naïve. Jeff was an attorney who was trained to win at all costs. The idea of compromising was in direct conflict with his desire to slay whatever was in front of him.

If you haven't already, you may encounter a "Jeff" in your workplace. Like me, you'll probably attempt to get this person to flex a bit. I can tell you from personal experience that you're about to go down a dead-end road. This person isn't going to change, which means you'll need to find another route to resolve the situation. Understand that there will be times where, no matter how hard you try, you're not going to reach an agreement on the next steps. While this will be disappointing, you may find comfort in knowing that this happens to everyone. When you get to this place, you're best off agreeing to disagree.

Knowing When to Stop Talking

The hardest part of any highly charged conversation is determining when the time has come to stop talking. This helps to explain why some people plow through these conversations, without so much as taking a breath. These people are more interested in getting the conversation behind them than they are in coming to a productive resolution. Don't be like them.

Take Time to Pause

If appropriate, follow this pause with a question that will allow the other person to catch up. For example, say you're telling your boss that you don't feel she is making use of your talent. Begin to state your case, pause, and ask, "Can you see why I might be feeling this way?" Then continue, after your boss has a chance to respond.

If you've written up a script to help you through a conversation, don't be afraid to include stage directions. Notes like "breath" or "pause" are good reminders of the need to slow down when approaching what undoubtedly will be some sharp curves in the conversation.

Get Comfortable with Silence

All of us have been in situations where the room suddenly gets silent. When this occurs, the first thing we tend to do is jump in and blurt something out. Yet, what may be best is to take in the silence. One of the most powerful tools in serious conversations is silence. If you know how and when to use silence in a conversation, it will elevate your relationships and every interaction you have at work, as well as at home.

Silence allows the other person time to go deeper. For example, let's say you're sharing something with someone, or they're telling you a story, and a moment of silence occurs. If this happens, nod your head and remain silent. Maintain eye contact, which will show the other party you're still engaged in the conversation. When both parties feel the other person is listening intently, the conversation will go deeper. After all, most people will do just about anything to fill the empty void that is silence.

Those that are deep thinkers will be grateful that you've given them the space they need to reflect so they can respond with a thoughtful reply. When you embrace silence, people will also see you as a great listener. Silence shows that you are taking time to think about your response—that you care. When people think you care about their well-being, they naturally care more about you, which in turn strengthens your relationship.

In the next chapter, we'll explore the principle of perception and why your behaviors matter more than your intentions. We'll be addressing the power of perception and steps you can take to ensure your behavior accurately reflects your intent.

KEY LEARNING POINTS

- Compromise is an agreement or a resolution of a dispute that is reached by each side making concessions.

- Unhealthy competition is about winning at all costs and is a losing strategy for resolving conflict. In comparison, compromise is a give-and-take proposition.

- Respect is something we all yearn for, and at times, it feels like it's in short supply in the workplace. Recognizing that difficult conversations may be more challenging for some people is the first step toward establishing a respectful relationship with someone who may not see things the way you do.

- When two people mutually respect each other, they'll continue the dialogue. The moment either party perceives disrespect, the conversation is no longer about the original topic.

- Disagreement isn't necessarily a bad thing—that is, if we can disagree productively. Disagreement usually comes down to one thing—perspective.

- When seeking common ground, focus on the why, keep your eyes on the prize, be open to all alternatives, and try to understand the other person's perspective.

- For a relationship to prosper, both parties must get something out of it. Each party must feel like they're being treated fairly.

- Influencing is asking for something you need in a way that allows the other person to say yes to whatever you've presented, which is exactly what we want someone to do when we're in the middle of a challenging conversation.

- The stronger your relationship is with someone, the easier it will be to influence this person. Without that relationship, the other person may view you as being manipulative.

- When you think about a difficult conversation, it's good to remember that the best path forward might involve a step back.

- You can reset the thermostat on a heated conversation by pulling back and reminding the other person what you're seeking to achieve.

- The hardest part of any highly charged conversation is determining when the time has come to stop talking. Get comfortable with silence, as some people are deep thinkers.

06

Credibility

*Recognizing That Your Word Is Only
as Good as Your Actions*

Credibility isn't a trait you're born with—it's something you have to earn day in and day out and is a critical component for productive conversations of any kind. In fact, without credibility, your words mean nothing, which is why I've chosen to include credibility as one of the seven principles for navigating difficult conversations at work. In this chapter, I'll be talking about what credibility means (and what it doesn't mean), the power of perception—why behaviors matter more than intentions, and whether or not it's possible to change perception. I'll be sharing some powerful habits for establishing credibility as a leader, as well as what you can do to reestablish credibility. The chapter will end with a discussion on establishing credibility with remote employees, as the work-from-home trend continues to gain in popularity.

What Credibility Is

One of the most important types of capital you can build at work is a reputation for being highly credible. Yet, we don't seem to pay much attention to how others perceive us. I'm as guilty as the next person in terms of ignoring this essential factor. I mentioned earlier that I was promoted to senior management at the age of twenty-four.

I was awarded all the perks that came with being the head of a department, including a corner office and a reserved parking spot. I mistakenly thought that credibility also came with my director title—similar to what happens when someone is crowned king or queen. I quickly discovered this was not the case.

I made a concerted effort to dress in a way that made me appear more mature, with the hopes this would boost my credibility, and soon realized that the only one I was kidding was myself. My peers (who were at least a decade or two older than me) still viewed me as a kid with no business experience and even less life experience. I guess you could say I was the poster child of a leader with zero credibility. Only at the time, I didn't know it. What people didn't realize was that I *did* have work experience. I'd been working since the age of thirteen and held several co-op positions while in college. I spent a little over two years working in HR before joining this company. I had experience in my field. Yet, no one seemed to care. What mattered most was their perception of me.

The first several years in this role were an uphill battle. I'd take one step forward and two steps backward. Eventually, I began to win over several of my peers. Yet, a few key members of the executive team were harder to bring over to my side. I knew I'd have to even the playing field for the others to view me as credible in this role. You see, just about every director had an advanced degree. After a year on the job, I applied and was accepted into the MBA program at the University of Houston. I felt I had to earn this MBA as quickly as possible, which is why I chose to plow through a four-year night program in two years. I nearly killed myself doing so, as I tried to balance the challenge of graduate school and working full-time.

While working on my MBA, I noticed that people started to treat me differently. They began to see me as a valued member of the executive team. No doubt, I was a bit smarter than I was before enrolling in this program. However, as I look back, the most significant change that occurred was how I showed up for work every day. The further along I got in earning my degree, the more self-assured I became. I projected an aura of confidence, which made a massive difference in how others perceived me. *I felt credible*, which was vital in getting people to view me as someone they could respect and trust.

Many people (including myself) have gone through or are currently experiencing something we call the imposter syndrome. You doubt your skills, talents, or accomplishments and are always worried that you'll be exposed as a fraud. It wasn't until much later in life that I realized that if you don't believe you deserve something, others won't think you are deserving either. As I look back on my career, I can see how I contributed to my credibility problem. Although on the surface I did believe I was deserving of being promoted to a director position and could do the job, deep down inside, I wondered if my peers were right. I felt like they were always waiting for me to fail. Subconsciously, I probably was as well.

Credibility is about being trusted and being perceived as believable. It's how you make people feel, which is why credibility starts with you. No one is going to believe in you when you don't believe in yourself. An example of this is on full display in one of my favorite movies—*The Wizard of Oz*. The Scarecrow wishes for a brain, the Cowardly Lion wants a dose of courage, and the Tin Man wants a heart. These characters are off to see the Wizard, only to discover they had what they were searching for all along. Over the years, I've met my share of "Scarecrows." These are people who believe they're not smart enough or that they're being discriminated against because they don't have a degree. The difference between these people and the Scarecrow is that the Scarecrow went searching for a solution. In my experience, people often complain about their circumstances and do little or nothing to change their condition. At some point, you have to take responsibility for your actions.

A company has the right to set the minimum standards for a particular job. People have the right to expect a certain level of education before seeing someone as credible and trusting them with their life. If a company (or the government) requires a four-year or an advanced degree for a particular position, then that's just the way it is. Despite what you may think about the value of a college education, most agree that a college degree is a credibility statement. Think about it. Would you be comfortable driving in a car engineered by a team of people without a formal education? Or taking a vaccine created by people who only had a high school degree? I wouldn't.

For many, getting a degree is a confidence builder. And who couldn't use an extra shot of confidence, especially when going head-to-head with someone who has more initials after his name than can fit on a business card? While writing this chapter, someone sent me a link to an article about a guy who never completed his college degree despite his smarts. He admitted that he used to complain a lot about not having his degree. So much so that his girlfriend once applied to a university on his behalf without telling him. He felt he had to work harder to prove himself to his employers. Although he never noticed any serious gap in his knowledge, he felt something was missing. He started to regret his decision to drop out of college. Years later, he enrolled in an online university and completed his degree in three months. He finished the thirty-four courses (120 credits) required for his computer science degree within this timeframe through grit and determination. His case is extreme. However, it does show that if you put your mind to something, you can get things done and that credibility starts with your belief in yourself.

Credibility is a judgment that the audience makes about how believable the communicator is. It's crucial in terms of communication because people often choose to respond to a persuasive message based not on the content but on their perception of the communicator. If someone in your organization suggests an idea and this person is credible, you'll be more accepting of what they are saying than if you don't perceive them as having much in terms of credibility. You may be new at your job and haven't had a chance yet to demonstrate your credibility. The good news is that credibility is a trait that's obtainable for all. With that in mind, here are some ways you can increase your standing and help with those difficult conversations.

Be Well-Read

Learn as much as you can about your field or the topic that you will be discussing. You know you will be heading into a meeting where the other party will probably challenge what you say. You may even have a good sense in terms of what precisely will be a sticking point. Do your research before the meeting, so you come across as credible.

I remember a particularly tough conversation that I had with my boss. I wanted to convince him to introduce a new employee benefit, which on the surface appeared like it would cost a lot of money. I arrived at our meeting with facts in hand and was glad I did. He pushed back hard. I didn't back down, presented him with the facts, and eventually he said yes to my request. I had proven to him that I had done my homework. I came across as credible.

Let's say I went into this meeting and wasn't well prepared. I would have presented my case, and when my boss pushed back, I would have stumbled to answer his questions. Any credibility that I might have had with him would have gone out the window. He may have even second-guessed why he had given me this job in the first place. One thing is for sure. He would have said no to my request, which would have made future discussions around resources even more complicated than they already were.

Be Consistent

Have you ever encountered someone whose work was inconsistent? I have. Her name was Judy. Somedays, her work was flawless, and other days it was like someone else was showing up in her place. We had several discussions about this. Yet, she consistently performed inconsistently. Her reputation for being an unpredictable performer resulted in her missing out on a promotion. I couldn't trust that she would be able to succeed in a more demanding role. She left the company soon after that.

It's our behaviors that matter—not our intentions. To up your credibility score, you'll need to be sure everything you say *and* do is consistent. Otherwise, people won't trust you, thereby making it difficult (if not impossible) to tackle tough work conversations. Here's a typical example of the damage inconsistency can have on one's credibility.

Imagine your company is going through some tough times. Earlier in the year, you tell the staff that everyone is taking a 10 percent reduction in pay. They later find out that several people were given a pass, and one person even got a raise. You now have to tell your employees there will be no year-end bonuses. You follow this up with a speech on how you hope they'll remain committed to the firm as you try to turn things around.

Save the lecture for someone who cares. You've already demonstrated that what you say and what you do are inconsistent. I've seen this routine before. One of my clients lost their star engineer because of a similar move. Simply stated, this person no longer trusted my client's word, as his behavior did not align with what he said. Remember, trust is required for others to view you as credible—especially when handling a difficult work situation. And if you don't have credibility with the person or people you are speaking with, you might as well save your breath.

Own Your Mistakes

No one expects you to be perfect. However, they do hope that you own up to it when you make a mistake and take steps to correct the error. Admitting mistakes, when done the right way, not only increases credibility but also increases reciprocity. Observing a leader taking full responsibility for a mistake, particularly when it's obvious the leader could have taken the easy way out or deflected criticism for their own benefit, encourages others to do the same when they commit an error.

We all know people who reactively say "sorry" more as a way to get someone off their case and to move conversations along quickly. After a while, their apology means nothing. If you've had a misstep and you're looking to save whatever credibility you have left, consider framing your conversation in a way that shows the other person you're taking responsibility for your share of the misunderstanding and that you're going to use this as a learning opportunity.

Here's how one of my past executive coaching clients apologized to his team for a business decision that ultimately cost the department a great deal of wasted time. His decision meant that the team had to work a bunch of unpaid overtime to recover. Rather than saying, "Sorry. I messed up. Thanks for your extra effort over the past several weeks," he said this instead: "Ultimately, the buck stops with me. I misjudged how long it would take for the supplier I chose to deliver on our order. I should have come to you when I realized we'd all have to work some nights and weekends to make up for lost time. I know better now and can assure you that I'll be much more communicative going forward. I apologize if my actions caused undue stress on you and your family." His team members reacted favorably to what he said. They realized he wasn't providing lip service. He truly was sorry and appeared to learn a valuable lesson from this whole experience.

He later confided in me that one of his employees came to him about a week later and apologized for a mistake they had made. They took full responsibility and shared what they had learned with him. Another manager might have fired this person for making such a costly error. My client knew firsthand how difficult it is to admit you've made an expensive mistake. He considered this experience as on-the-job training and reaffirmed how appreciative he was that this employee had been forthright. It seemed this employee was not only listening to my client's apology—he was also watching and took what he saw to heart.

What Credibility Is Not

Credibility isn't something you can simply put on when you sense the conditions will call for another layer of trustworthiness. Nor is it something that you can pull off the shelf when you need it. It takes considerable time to establish credibility, which is why it's essential to work on your standing daily.

Some job titles like CEO, VP, Doctor, or Nurse come with a dose of credibility. However, a title alone does not make the man or the woman. There are many examples of professionals with big titles who have fallen from grace. Enron CEO Kenneth Lay and Theranos CEO Elizabeth Holmes are two people who immediately come to mind. There are also everyday leaders whose trustworthiness dissipated rapidly after assuming a high-level position. Many believe they still have credibility based on their job title when they don't. They haven't earned the trust of the people they serve. The truth is we're not very forgiving, especially when people haven't made much in terms of deposits into the bank of trust. When a leader slips up and loses his or her people's confidence, we're not incredibly patient for individuals to rehabilitate themselves. Here's one such example.

A former client of mine, by the name of John, was promoted to COO. He was a hardworking guy who worked his way up in the organization and was relatively well-liked and trusted until he reached the executive suite. His peers confided in me that they noticed a shift in John's attitude, which happened around the same time as his promotion. His employees noticed this as well. John went from being seen as an open and honest communicator to someone who appeared to be holding information back. At times, he seemed to use his position of power to get things done. When questioned about a particular operations matter, he would respond by saying, "Because I said so," or "Why are you questioning me? I'm the COO." His constant reminder to people about his title was tiresome. After a while, people began to lose faith in John. Things went from bad to worse when an operations error came to light on a project he was spearheading. In the past, people would have rallied around John and done anything to ensure he looked good. Not anymore. They lost faith in him and were happy to stand by while his boat sank. John's fatal mistake was thinking his title carried enough clout to excuse his dismissive behavior toward others. It didn't.

John was fortunate to have still one ally left in the company—the CEO, who engaged me to help John reach a place of redemption. First, I had to hold the mirror up so that John could see how others were viewing him in the organization. He honestly had no idea his behavior was hurting his credibility. Admittedly, we had a few "tough love" sessions but eventually he came around. He went directly to his peers and team members and apologized for what he had done. He asked for their forgiveness and promised to do better. He told them he was working with an executive coach to help him change some behaviors that were not serving him or the organization well and even asked a few of them to participate in the process. It took John over six months to shift his behavior and become more like his former self. He told me he was amazed at how quickly one can fall from grace and was grateful his CEO was there to catch him.

John is not the same guy he was when we started working together. He's more humble and understands that with a title comes great responsibility. Titles also come with expected behavior and explicit and unspoken promises. As a leader, your actions are visible. If you prefer to remain invisible, then consider remaining an individual contributor.

The Power of Perception

People judge us all the time based on their understanding, which is why it's critical to be aware of how people perceive you and manage perceptions. People often have different perceptions of the same reality. It's not uncommon for one party to think they're right and that the other person is wrong. Or that they're not the problem—the other person is.

We have different perceptions about the same situation because we have different life experiences that shape how we see things. We may also not have access to the same information. This helps to explain why, when faced with a difficult conversation, people often jump to conclusions. We think we know what the other person will say, based on what we would say, so we don't listen very carefully. Instead, we're busy preparing our response. Or we immediately assume bad intent because of a similar incident that occurred with someone else. When this happens, the conversation quickly goes off the rails, and it's hard for both parties to get back on track.

People are continually evaluating us based on our behavior. They're asking themselves questions like "Is this person credible?" "Are they telling me the truth or what they think I want to hear?" "Can I trust them?" How someone answers these questions is based on how they view the person they're speaking with and their experience in similar situations. It's hard to ignore your own perception. However, what if we took this one step further, before entering into a demanding work conversation, and asked ourselves similar questions from a different perspective? What if we were to reframe the questions and instead ask ourselves, "How credible am I coming across to this other person?" "Have I given them any reason to doubt I'm being completely transparent?" "Have I given them cause not to trust me?" Don't worry if you don't know the answers to all these questions. You may decide to explore this further, should you find you hit a dead end when addressing a high-stakes situation.

Here's an example of using these types of questions to overcome barriers you may encounter in uncomfortable discussions at work, when you think the other person may see you differently than you see yourself. I've never been one to beat around the bush and believe it's best to call out the elephant in the room. Earlier in my career, I had to have one of those difficult conversations with the company receptionist regarding appropriate office attire. Here's how it went.

Me: You may not realize this, but what you're wearing is completely inappropriate for the office. This is an office where how you present yourself matters, especially when you're the first person clients see when they enter our suite.

Receptionist: What's wrong with what I'm wearing?

Me (thinking, really?): I know the vibe in every office is different. What's appropriate work attire for one company isn't necessarily appropriate for another. Here we lean toward the conservative side, as we service high-net-worth individuals and institutions. A more tailored look is what's appropriate here.

Receptionist: Well, I'm going out directly after work and won't have time to change, so I thought it was okay to wear this.

Me: I get how this dress thing can be confusing. Someone had a similar conversation with me when I was starting out, and I was grateful.

Receptionist: I think I'm dressed fine.

Me: Look, have I ever given you a reason not to trust me? I want you to have an opportunity to move up here. I wouldn't be taking the time to address this with you if I didn't think you had potential.

The breakthrough moment for our conversation occurred when I asked her if I had ever given her reason not to trust me. You see, earlier in the year, I helped her out of a jam. I thought I had built enough trust with her to address this uncomfortable situation. As the conversation continued, I got the sense that I may have overestimated how much of a trusting relationship we had. The only way to know this for sure, was to ask, which I did. The question, "Have I ever given you a reason not to trust me?" resulted in a pause. It was at this moment that the receptionist stopped to consider where I was coming from. The tone of the conversation changed noticeably as she came to realize I was trying to support her. It was like we hit the reset button. We spent the remainder of our time discussing affordable stores where young professional women typically shop.

People waste a great deal of time and energy skirting around issues when trying to resolve differences of opinion. When I see this happening with a client, I ask, "Why are you going around the block when the answer is next door?" This usually gets their attention. Direct communication and calling things as you see them will help you arrive at your conversation destination a lot quicker than beating around the bush. It will also enhance your credibility, as people won't be second-guessing your authenticity.

The only way to know exactly how someone perceives a particular situation is to ask. You can do this by saying something like, "We seem to see things very differently. Here's my take on what's going on here. What's yours?" It's challenging to change people's perceptions, which we'll talk about more in the following section. However, it's nearly impossible to do so when you don't have a clue as to where they're coming from. When in doubt, ask!

Reading the Room: Is Your Credibility on the Decline?

Credibility is built on a foundation of confidence in the other person and ethical behavior. In fact, according to the Edelman Trust Barometer 2020, ethical drivers are three times more critical to company trust than competence.[1] Taking this one step further, integrity is the top driver on the list, followed by dependability and purpose. People don't work for companies—they work for people, so it would stand to reason that the factors survey respondents are noting are about company leadership. Another interesting takeaway from this report is who experts and peers view as being most credible in an organization. Company technical experts received a score of 68 percent, while CEOs and successful entrepreneurs scored much lower on the scale—both coming in at 47 percent.

So, how do you figure out where you rate in terms of trust and credibility when you don't have the resources for a formal 360-degree assessment conducted on your behalf? A 360-degree assessment is where the manager, peers, and direct reports are asked to provide feedback regarding behaviors they can see. You can still ask people in your organization for feedback. Table 6.1 shows a quick and easy credibility assessment tool you can use to collect this information. I recommend you ask for feedback using this credibility assessment biannually. This way, if your credibility begins to wane, you can put corrections into place before it's too late.

Now that you know where you stand in terms of your credibility, here are some signs that may indicate your credibility could be on the decline and how you can boost it.

People No Longer Confide in You

Your staff or even your boss used to confide in you. They no longer do. People confide in people with whom they feel comfortable. Try to identify exactly when you began to notice this shift in behavior. Was it when you were asked to take on additional responsibilities at work that resulted in you no longer having time to chat with people? Did something happen that left someone feeling like you might have breached confidentiality? Identifying when this change began to happen may help you get back on track and build your credibility back up. You may still owe someone an apology. If this is the case, here's a way to handle the conversation.

You: The thought has occurred to me that something has changed in our relationship. You used to confide in me, and you no longer do. Have I done something to make you no longer trust me?

TABLE 6.1   CREDIBILITY ASSESSMENT

Please rate me in each of the following areas	4 = All the time 3 = Most times 2 = Sometimes 1 = Rarely 0 = Never N/A = Not Applicable
Ability to admit mistakes.	☐
Willingness to offer apologies when I'm wrong.	☐
Willingness to right wrongs.	☐
Keeping you in the loop.	☐
Candor when delivering news that is either good or bad.	☐
Commitment to supporting you in your career aspirations.	☐
Honesty when answering tough questions.	☐
Doing what I say I will do.	☐
Responding to your questions in a timely manner.	☐
Thoughtful responses to your questions.	☐
Willingness to admit when I don't know something.	☐
Authenticity in terms of my leadership.	☐

NOTE Any area with a score of 2 or lower requires immediate attention.

Your boss: Well, I'm glad you brought this up. Several weeks ago, I shared something with you in confidence. I later found out that you told someone.

You: I'm not sure what exactly you're talking about. Can you be more specific?

Your boss: Yes. I told you that we might have to make some staff cuts. A day later, one of your employees came to me asking if his job was secure.

You: Oh. I can see why you might have thought that I broke your confidence. Here's what happened. Right after our conversation, one of my employees came to me and told me he would be putting an offer in to buy a house. As you know, it's public knowledge that our revenues are down and that we've had a challenging year. I reminded him of this and suggested that he wait before making a significant purchase. However, I can certainly see why you might have thought that I shared highly confidential information. I hope this explanation will allow us to get back on track.

Your boss: Yes, I'm relieved to hear this was merely a misunderstanding. Thanks for coming in and talking with me about this.

You're No Longer Seen as the "Go-To" Guy or Gal

You used to be the first person people came to for counsel. This is no longer the case. You've made some careless mistakes in the past and didn't realize the damage this has done to your credibility. Here's how you might want to handle this conversation with a coworker.

You: It seems like I was the first person team members called upon to troubleshoot a problem. Honestly, I can't remember the last time that's happened. What gives?

Coworker: If we're being honest here, your work is no longer reliable. We have to check and double-check your drawings, which creates way more work than it's worth.

You: You're right. I've been distracted. Do you think there's a way I can earn back your trust?

Coworker: I'm not going to make any promises here. You'll have to earn our trust back.

You: That's fair. Let's start right now.

You're Passed Up for a Promotion

You thought you had this promotion locked in, only to find it went to someone else. How on earth could this possibly have happened? People are promoted based on performance and potential. Somewhere along the line, you may have lost credibility. It's best to find out now to prevent this from happening again. Here's where to begin.

You: I don't understand. I thought for sure I was the obvious choice for this promotion.

Your boss: You might have been six months ago, but not anymore.

You: What do you mean?

Your boss: Over the past few months, I've given you several opportunities to present to the leadership team. You did what was asked of you and nothing more. Simply put, you didn't impress anyone.

You: Can you say more?

Your boss: When you first arrived here, you were quickly identified as a high-potential, meaning we expected great things from you. We talked about this at great length at your mid-year performance review meeting. Your recent performance at the last leadership meeting was less than stellar, while your colleague hit a home run. The leadership team agreed she was the right choice for this promotion.

You: That's unfortunate. What do I need to focus on to prove I'm ready to take on more responsibility in the future?

Your boss: That's a more extended conversation than time permits right now. Let's put this on the agenda for our weekly meeting. In the meantime, let's both give this some thought.

There's no escaping it. Demonstrating competence is vital for credibility. You might think someone is sincere and honest, but you won't trust this person entirely if they don't get *consistent* results. Inconsistency, whether it's keeping your word sometimes and not others or in terms of performance, can be one of the fastest ways to see your credibility plummet. Challenging work conversations are made even more complicated when we're speaking with someone who lacks credibility. Through some miracle, you may come to a mutually agreed-upon resolution. However, in all likelihood, the follow-through required to make this promise a reality is highly unlikely to happen.

Changing Perception: Can It Be Done?

I'm often asked if it's possible to change perception. I guess that depends on your perspective. Here's a story about a former client who, despite her impressive education and her flawless work record, still wasn't being taken seriously by her peers or her company.

Earlier in my career, I left my company to work for another organization, where I worked my way up to an executive position. Years later, I returned to my company in a director role. On my six-year anniversary, I decided to approach our new human resources director to talk about my desire to return to an executive-level position. When I did, he shared an interesting point with me.

He said, "Many people still see you as the person who started here on the line. These guys started there as well. However, they've moved up in the organization together. You, on the other hand, left the company. They don't have a clue what you did while you were gone. All they know is that you've returned to the company to lead a global program." I asked, "So, what am I supposed to do?" He said, "You need to change their perception of you."

People's perceptions are their own reality. I learned this through training on behavioral traits. No outside influence can change perception. The person must be willing to consider a new reality. I asked him a question to ensure I had heard right. "So, what you are telling me is I must change their perception of me?" He said, "Yes, that is exactly what I need you to do, in order for me to help you advance your career here."

This realization was heart-wrenching. For years I showed my credibility as a leader by launching many global programs and doing so successfully. People who didn't really know me or what I was capable of were the same people who would prevent my growth. My choice was clear; a new start building new perceptions would be what I needed to advance my career. I left the company soon thereafter.

Jacqueline MacPherson, PhD
Associate director, Engineering-Processing and Packaging
Nice-Pak Products, Inc.

Changing perception is hard—I mean really hard. However, you *can* change people's perception of you. I know this because most of the coaching work I do with executives helps them change behaviors while changing their stakeholders' perceptions. It takes tremendous discipline for someone to successfully alter the way people view them as well as a keen desire to do so. Patience is also required, as it can take months—sometimes even a year—to change perception. That's because for some, a shift in behavior is temporary. We all know people who say they're going to alter a particular behavior—like smoking. They start off strong, and everyone is proud of them. Three months later, we see them sneaking out the back door to grab a smoke. The next time they tell us they're going to quit smoking, we say to ourselves, "Yeah, right!" People believe what they see, hear, and feel. In order to change perception, you have to sustain your new behaviors. Only then will people believe that your word is as good as your actions.

The HR director at Jacqueline's company was spot-on—she needed to change how she was being perceived. However, there are situations where the effort required to alter perception far outweighs the benefits. I know Jacqueline and am aware of the culture at that organization. She was one of a handful of women working in a male-dominated company and was never treated as an equal, despite having a PhD, which few people in the company had. The amount of energy she would have had to exert to change even one person's perception of her would not have been worth the effort. Given the situation, the decision to build new perceptions elsewhere was the right thing for her to do. I recently spoke to Jacqueline, and she is now working for a company that is thrilled to have her. She's well respected by her peers, who are still mostly male.

Let's say Jacqueline had worked at a company where making an effort to change perception would have been worth the effort. I would have suggested that she ask the HR director (or an outside party) to facilitate a 360-degree assessment. The 360-degree assessment report would have given Jacqueline insight in terms of exactly how she was being perceived. Next, I would have suggested that Jacqueline select one or two behaviors that were holding her back and commit to changing those behaviors. I would have recommended that she reach out to her stakeholders (some of whom are part of the group that moved up while she was gone) to tell them what she was working on and ask for their help. Together, they'd come up with an action plan. The stakeholders would be there to help keep her accountable. Facing the issue head-on and asking for guidance while working on self-improvements is part of the Stakeholder Centered Coaching approach that I use with my coaching clients. Over the years, I have found this methodology to be one of the most effective ways to change perception in the workplace. Stakeholders are more than willing to help someone who publicly states they want to be helped, and often, these people wind up being this person's biggest advocate.

In some situations, too much damage has already been done to ever change perception. An example of this is when McDonald's discovered that former CEO Steve Easterbrook had violated company policy by engaging in a consensual relationship with an employee. The fast-food giant said he had demonstrated poor judgment and that McDonald's forbids managers from having romantic relationships with direct or indirect subordinates. Easterbrook was fired. It was later revealed, in a lawsuit filed by MacDonald's against Easterbrook, that there was even more to the story than initially stated, including allegations of physical, sexual relationships with three McDonald's employees in the year before his termination, and approval of hundreds of thousands of dollars in stock grants for one of those employees during their sexual relationship.

No amount of coaching will have any impact on how people perceive the Easterbrooks of the world. Save your breath. If you've got someone in the organization who is radioactive, it's best to cut your losses. Do so before this individual does any more damage.

Establishing Credibility with Remote Employees

It's harder to establish credibility with people you don't regularly see than it is for people you see daily. However, it's not impossible. Sometimes it's easier to do so when you're all in the same boat.

When the coronavirus pandemic first hit back in 2020, many people (including myself) wondered how they'd be able to build relationships with coworkers and customers when the majority of people were working from home. Most of us struggled to figure out how to engage people who were not physically in the room with us. The fact that we were going through similar challenges made it a bit easier to build rapport and credibility. We were all learning together. People seemed more forgiving, and no one was expecting perfection.

We quickly learned we needed to be more intentional in our actions and communication if we were to be successful in establishing and retaining credibility with an entire workforce we could suddenly no longer see. It took a while for us to figure this out. Here are some of the key takeaways that we're now using to do a better job of building rapport and credibility in the remote world of work. These suggestions will help you, as an employee, establish and retain credibility.

Webcams On

I get that some people don't like to have their video cameras on when they're on Zoom calls. That's fine sometimes, but not all of the time. Using webcams to put faces to names allows participants to grow familiarity, connection, and trust among you and other team members. If you're running the meeting, let people know you expect them to turn on their webcams.

Double Down on Communication

The saying "Out of sight, out of mind" rings true. When you're working remotely, your boss has no idea if you're actually working or if you are out running errands. It's essential for remote workers to frequently communicate with their boss and remind them about their contribution.

If you haven't done so already, consider setting up a fifteen-minute weekly check-in call with your boss or your people to ensure you're staying in touch with one another. Few things become more damaging to trust among virtual workers than the feeling that employees are "kept out of the loop," especially when it comes to important decisions. Be sure you're looping in your virtual workers on strategic choices, personnel changes, and other important company announcements. Doing so will help you to build and maintain trust and credibility with your staff.

Adhere to Response Times

We've talked a lot about credibility and the importance of doing what you say you will do. Adhering to response times goes a long way in building trust. It can be a lot more time consuming to track someone down when they're located several miles or time zones away from you than when this person is working on your floor. If you see you're not going to make a particular deadline, let the other person know right away that you require more time.

Choose the Right Outlet for Communication

Companies seem to offer a variety of communication channels. Pick the most appropriate one based on your objectives and what you're trying to communicate. For example, tools like Microsoft Teams, Skype, or Zoom for video are great for rapport building. Slack, Basecamp, and plain old Text are terrific ways to keep in touch with team members without interrupting them. And of course, there is the telephone, which many people forget is still an option.

Leaders should show their employees appreciation. My son Zach is working remotely as a co-op employee and recently received a surprise from his employer—a company swag gift certificate. Another remote worker I know, Dan, says that occasionally his manager ships him office supplies for no reason. Now and again, he throws in a few bags of Dan's favorite snack food, along with a note saying things like, "I know how hard you're working on the company website. I'm sending you snacks to ensure you don't go hungry." Dan says it feels good to know that his boss is looking out for him. He likes the notes the most, as they remind him that he's not alone and that his boss is aware of his efforts.

One of my clients paid for a subscription meal delivery service for her remote workers. She knows how stressful it can be to plan and cook meals while you're working from home and under some fairly tight deadlines. She hopes this surprise gift will make her employees' evenings a little more enjoyable.

Occasional acts of appreciation and notes of gratitude show employees that you value them and go a long way toward establishing a trusting relationship with your team members and will increase your credibility with them, no matter where they reside. Don't fret about whether your way of showing appreciation is the right way to do so. It's the act of showing gratitude that matters the most.

The next chapter is on courage, which is the seventh principle of *Can We Talk?* We'll be looking at some of the more challenging work scenarios and conversations that may require a dose of nerve to muster through.

KEY LEARNING POINTS

- Credibility isn't a trait you're born with—it's something you have to earn day in and day out.

- Credibility is about being trusted and being perceived as believable.

- When you project confidence, you come across as more credible.

- You can increase your standing, which will help you more easily navigate difficult conversations by being well-read, being consistent, and owning your mistakes.

- It's our behaviors that matter—not our intentions.

- People judge us based on their understanding, which is why it's critical to be aware of how people perceive you and manage those perceptions.

- People don't work for companies. They work for people and will remain with those they trust.

- Changing perception is hard, but can be done. It takes discipline to successfully alter the way people view you and a keen desire to do so.

- It takes more effort to establish credibility with people you don't regularly see than with people you see daily. Keep webcams on, double down on communication, and remember to demonstrate your appreciation for remote team members.

Endnote

1 Global report: Edelman trust barometer 2020, Edelman, December 2020, cdn2.hubspot.net/hubfs/440941/Trust%20Barometer%202020/2020%20 Edelman%20Trust%20Barometer%20Global%20Report.pdf?utm_ campaign=Global:%20Trust%20Barometer%202020&utm_source=Website (archived at https://perma.cc/44M9-NUPE)

07

Courage

Navigating the Obstacles

I've chosen courage as one of the seven principles for navigating difficult conversations at work because high-stakes conversation often require a dose of this. The fact that this principle is last doesn't make it any less important than the others. In this chapter, I'll be covering why it's important to have the courage of your talent and provide guidance on how to get comfortable with discomfort. I'll also be discussing one of my favorite subjects—office politics—a topic many would prefer to ignore. I'm aiming to help you improve your ability to swiftly navigate through some highly charged political work situations and will be providing guidance to help you choose your office battles wisely. We'll end the chapter with a discussion on how to muster up the courage to take your power back when you seem to have inadvertently given it away.

The Courage of Your Talent

Have you ever done something that you thought was unimpressive and had people say, "Wow! That took a lot of courage" or "You're really brave. I could never do that"? You may have thought to yourself, "Why are they making such a big deal out of this?" That's because taking courageous action may look different for people in different situations. For example, I do a lot of public speaking and have spoken to audiences with more than 500 people in the room. Speaking in front of large groups has never worried me. I told this to a friend, a doctor who confided in me that she gets nervous if she has to present at a small meeting. She then went on to say how she thought I was brave. Yet, I look at her and often wonder where she gets the courage to work with sick patients, day in and day out. That's something I could never do.

Courage is the determination to move forward despite the fear. It's more than a mindset or an emotion. It's a principle of action. You muster up the nerve to do something, even though it might frighten you. One of my most memorable moments of courage happened the first time I participated in a night dive in Turks and Caicos. I was quite nervous, as I wasn't a very experienced scuba diver. However, I felt I needed to give it a try, as I had heard such wonderful stories about the experience. I remember the divemaster giving us the sign that it was time to go and me thinking, "I'm not ready!"

I somehow mustered up the courage and jumped off the side of the boat. About a minute into the dive, I felt someone take my hand. Together, we descended and enjoyed the fantastic scenery around us. I felt calm and at peace. When we returned to the boat, I heard a couple arguing. She was saying to her partner, "You promised to hold my hand." And he was exclaiming, "I did!" I couldn't help but smile when I realized this was the guy who had held my hand. It seems that in the dark ocean, he had mistaken me for his partner. This experience taught me two things. When faced with adversity, I have the power to choose whether to dive right in or let fear keep me back. It also made me realize that our worries can be eased when there is someone by our side. I hope to be that someone for you as you find your courage and address those tough work conversations you know you need to have.

I often remind clients that they need to have the courage of their talent. All of us are talented in one way or another. Yet, fear holds us back from undertaking what we're capable of doing or saying what needs to be said. Granted, in business, courage seldom resembles the heroic actions that occur in life-or-death situations or Hollywood movies. However, this doesn't make tough work conversations any less scary or courageous. The next time you hesitate to do or say something out of fear, I want you to remember the phrase "the courage of your talent." When you find yourself in one of these situations, take a few moments to remind yourself of your superpowers. For some of you, this may be your ability to bounce back quickly from setbacks or your knack for de-escalating heated discussions. For others, this could be your gift of being able to remain calm in any situation. Next, weigh the risks against the benefits. What's the worst thing that can happen if you proceed with this conversation, and what outcomes might you miss out on if you choose to remain silent? You'll find that quite often, the risks aren't as high as you initially thought they were and that the benefits are many. Gather your courage and take action. The more you face your fears, the easier it will be to do so in the future.

The following is an example of two people having what turned out to be an unplanned courageous conversation. Both parties used the courage of their talent to say what needed to be said.

Years ago, I was hired for an extremely well-known anti-virus software company and worked for a genius, Wharton School of Business, suit and tie, smooth-talking CEO, who replaced the crazy (and now very well known) founder/ex-CEO, where my responsibilities included overseeing our corporate meetings. It was an outrageous ride—and I haven't experienced anything like it since. We learned from the top to take no prisoners, just do it, and ask forgiveness later. Our CEO's famous quote was "drive fast, take chances."

One particular event still haunts me. I was planning a major international conference at the El Conquistador Hotel. The logistics of this were tremendous, from arrivals to ground transportation, welcome gifts, staging, lighting, presentations, and food. In the middle of setting up the event, I started getting calls from the front desk that people checking in had the wrong arrival dates and rooms weren't ready. I couldn't understand how this could be, as my trusted employee (who had become a dear friend) and I went over this list a hundred times.

I called her on our walkie-talkies, and we met upstairs with my hotel contact to figure out what went wrong. I said to my trusted employee,

"Why is the front desk constantly calling me regarding the arrivals? This was the one task I gave you to take care of." I stared and stared at the list and then realized that she had deleted a few rows on the Excel sheet, which resulted in her altering the dates of all 600 arrivals on the list!

I started screaming in the lobby at her, "This is not a good sign starting off the program like this. Everyone is assigned their individual tasks, and yours fell short right out of the gate!" I kicked a plant and almost broke a glass table—I just lost it. I told her to pack her bags and to get on the first plane flight back to California. In anger, I then said, "Are you stupid or just incompetent? Never mind... I know the answer to that," and she started crying—it was a mess. I left and went to the ballroom and finished my work there, just fuming.

Two hours later, she found me and asked, "Can we talk?" I looked at her and just shook my head and said, "I'm done." She then said with tears in her eyes, "This is the hardest conversation I've ever had, but after this trip, I don't want to work for you anymore. I value your friendship way too much, and it's more important to me for you to remain my friend than to travel around the world and work for you." I hugged her and said, "I'm so, so sorry. I know I can be hard to work for, and you truly are an exceptional employee and even a better friend. I value your friendship so whatever you decide is fine with me."

After that, I learned not to be so much like my CEO. People make mistakes, and everything can't always be perfect, especially people. Now in my sixties, I realize there is no perfection in life, and I thank this employee, who has become a lifelong friend, for opening my eyes to this.

Andrea Nation
Executive Assistant to CEO
Drishti

I see several examples of the courage of one's talent here. Clearly the employee who deleted a few rows of the Excel spreadsheet made a mistake—one that caused considerable stress for all parties involved. It took a lot of courage for her to show her face in the ballroom again and to tell her boss that she was choosing friendship over her job. She weighed the benefits of remaining silent or speaking up and chose to engage her boss in a conversation.

While at first glance, it might not appear that her boss showed courage as well, she actually did. The first thought that went through my mind when Andrea shared this story with me was how brave she was to openly share a story that clearly wasn't one of her best moments. Could she have handled this situation better? Sure. However, Andrea was under immense pressure, which showed. As soon as she calmed down, Andrea realized her mistake of taking her employee to task in front of others. She found a way to set her ego aside and apologize. In my twenty-plus years of working inside organizations, I've never had a boss apologize to me, although there were certainly times when an apology was warranted. These managers didn't have the courage that Andrea had—admitting when they were wrong and asking for forgiveness. Is there someone at work to whom you owe an apology? If so, now would be a good time to take responsibility for your actions and make amends.

Getting Comfortable with Discomfort

I'd be lying if I told you I was extremely comfortable with discomfort. However, over the years, I've certainly become more comfortable with situations that used to make me uneasy. For example, I used to cringe at the thought of having to push back when I felt I wasn't being treated fairly. I'd ask myself, "Do you really want to make waves here?" Or I'd say to myself, "This is going to be very uncomfortable. I'm not sure I want to do this." I know now that if you don't advocate for yourself, no one else will, and I no longer hesitate to express how I feel about a particular situation, even if doing so might make the other person feel a bit uneasy. I used to hesitate to speak up when someone else presented one of my ideas as their own. I no longer do this. Experience has taught me the importance of addressing worrisome situations head-on and what happens when you pretend nothing is wrong. Admittedly, it's taken me twenty years to get here! My goal is to accelerate your learning so that it doesn't take you as long as it's taken me to get comfortable with discomfort.

Lots of people think that by *not* taking action, they'll be able to avoid discomfort. However, not taking action is a decision that can result in things remaining the same or worsening. So, the way I see it, you've got nothing to lose by attempting to resolve whatever discomfort you may be feeling.

There are those people who overthink everything and find themselves stuck in quicksand. When asked about their inertia, they'll tell you they need more time to do research, which if you think about it, is the *last* thing they need to do. Look, we'd all like to have a crystal ball that allows us to see into the future so that we could be 100 percent sure that our next move is the right move. As far as I know, no such item is available—at least not yet. We have to deal with the here and now and work with what we've got.

The best way to deal with discomfort is to take on a small task to help get the ball rolling. Taking on a simple action item, such as setting up a meeting date, can propel a conversation forward—nothing like a deadline to get you moving! Once you're in motion, you'll see more clearly what your next steps should be. You won't feel so overwhelmed and might even feel some sense of relief knowing that you're addressing a situation that's been weighing you down.

An exercise worth doing is to think about a time at work when you were very comfortable in your role. You might have been in a job that you could do with your eyes closed. You knew exactly what would occur the next day, as nothing ever changed. Jot down how you felt when you were in this situation.

Now, think about a time when you were in a job that wasn't all that predictable. One day you'd be working on a particular project, and then the next day, you might be flying to one of the satellite offices to put out a fire that was raging. Write down what it felt like when your job was less predictable.

My guess is that you experienced considerably more growth and career satisfaction when you were in the job where every day was unpredictable. There was no script to follow. You had to make things up as you went along. As a result, you experienced personal growth that wouldn't have occurred had you remained in a role where everything always went according to plan. You may not even have realized it at the time, but you became comfortable with discomfort. Think about this the next time you find yourself avoiding a situation because it makes you feel uncomfortable. Then push forward.

There will be times when no matter how comfortable you are with discomfort, you'll face a situation that shakes you to the core. Here's one such example.

During the second week of March 2020, I had to lay off seven of my nine employees due to the coronavirus. In the weeks prior, I spent many a night talking with my spouse, trying to come up with ways to reinvent my business so we wouldn't have to let people go. I finally realized that the only way we'd stand a chance of surviving, in the long run, was to make drastic short-term cuts.

It was the hardest thing I had to do in nineteen years of owning QRST's. Yes, I had to fire people over the years, but this was different. No one had done anything wrong. These folks showed up on time, did their work, and were a pleasure to have around.

I think everyone knew the layoff was coming. Work orders were slowing down, and we were all talking about the impact the virus was having on the economy, especially our business.

I gathered everyone up and said, "I've looked at our business from all angles, and the only way I can see this business still standing when this pandemic is over is for me to reduce the payroll." With tears about to flow from my eyes, I then said, "As of 4:00 p.m. today, I need to lay all of you off." There was silence in the room. Then, one by one, employees started to ask questions like, "When do you think we'll be called back?" and "When do you anticipate orders coming in again?" I gave them the only honest answer I could. I said, "I don't know."

It was almost three and a half months before I could bring everyone back, and when I did, their return to work was covered by one of the major Boston television stations. Our story was one of hope and survival when this was greatly needed in our country. As for me, I learned that you have to summon up the courage to do what needs to be done, no matter how uncomfortable doing so may feel for you. Had I not mustered up the courage to lay these people off, my company would most likely not be viable today, and many of my employees might still be unemployed.

Peter Rinnig
Owner
QRST's

Over the years, I've been a strategic advisor on talent to Peter and have found him to be a thoughtful leader who likes to be 100 percent sure he's making the right move before taking action on HR-related matters. Like many business owners during the pandemic, Peter found himself in a situation where he had to do something he never imagined—laying off the majority of his employees. Somehow, Peter found the strength to do what needed to be done. He did exactly as I would have advised. He prepared what he was going to say before calling his people together. He was brief and allowed the meeting to continue until everyone had a chance to ask questions. Most importantly, he was honest. He wasn't afraid to say, "I don't know" when he didn't have an answer.

When called back, all of Peter's employees returned, which didn't happen for all employers. At the time, there were additional government unemployment benefits being given out, making it possible to make more money staying home than if someone returned to work. Peter's willingness to have an open and honest conversation with his staff contributed to his people wanting to be there for him when business picked up.

None of us know how strong we are until we're faced with adversity. Hopefully this will be the last test in resiliency that Peter will have to go through for a while.

Office Politics: Navigating Highly Charged Conversations

Some of the most courageous conversations I've coached clients through were in highly political work environments. It takes a great deal of courage to have these difficult office politics conversations. I'm sharing examples of some of the highly politically charged conversations you may encounter to help you muster up the fortitude to take these situations on when they arise. In many cases, I had to point out to my clients that workplace politics was going on around them before proceeding. You see, lots of people think that if they keep their head down, they can avoid office politics. That's not how this works. No matter what others might tell you, office politics is one game that is played in *every* organization. It doesn't matter whether you work for a nonprofit, government agency, private company, or family-owned business, there is always a round of politics being played somewhere, which is why, if you ignore it, you do so at your own peril.

Before you begin writing your letter of resignation, it's essential to understand that politics isn't just about manipulation. It's about using power effectively. I'm a huge fan of Dr. Jeffrey Pfeffer's work on power and politics. His book *Managing with Power: Politics and Influence in Organizations* (1992) is as relevant today as the day it was written. Pfeffer defines power as the ability to get things done through other people. People who wield power effectively follow unwritten rules that allow them to maneuver swiftly through the organization to obtain scarce resources, approval of prized projects, and promotions. For our purposes, we're going to focus on some of the more challenging political conversations you may face at work. However, if you'd like more information on the topic of office politics, take a look at my book *Suddenly in Charge* (2017), where I dedicate an entire chapter to this important subject.

Here are some of the more common highly politically charged conversations you're bound to encounter.

The Almighty Fight for Headcount

The one big ask people struggle with is requesting additional head-count for their department. Many people don't realize how politically charged these conversations can get, especially when budgets are tight. Here's why this is so. Let's say you and I both want to add a person to our staff, and our boss tells us there's only enough money for one hire. For one of us to win, the other has to lose. Who will come out on top depends on several factors, including how politically astute we are and how convincing an argument we can make. When dealing with a situation like this, ask yourself, "What would be the benefit to my supervisor in saying yes to my request?" Knowing this will help you secure the resources you need.

Here are two ways to approach this conversation. The first example is how people typically go about asking for more staff. The second approach is used by people who are more politically savvy.

You: I'd like to hire another person for our team.

Your boss: Why do you think you need additional staff?

You: My people have been working a lot of hours just to keep up with what we have on our plate.

Your boss: Let's go over the projects you're currently working on and prioritize what's most important.

You: Okay. But how about the extra person I'd like to hire?

Your boss: As you pointed out, this would be an extra hire, which we don't have the budget for.

Now imagine if you approached the conversation from the position of how your request would best benefit your boss.

You: I know website security is one of your top priorities, given the recent security breach that occurred with our competitor.

Your boss: Yes, this is most certainly my number one priority, as our CEO made it very clear to me that this best not happen on my dime.

You: Well, I've been analyzing our current systems, and we may have some areas of vulnerability. To fix this and keep our systems safe, I'd like to bring on a chief security officer to oversee cybersecurity. In fact, I have someone in mind.

Your boss: Well, I'm sure our competitor wished they had done this before their data breach occurred. Let me talk to the CEO and see if I can get these funds approved.

Firing Someone You Don't Want to Fire

If you're in a management role long enough, there may come a day when your boss tells you to fire someone whom you don't believe should be let go. This is a tough conversation to have, even for seasoned leaders. First, you have to figure out if this is a battle worth fighting. In this scenario, the VP of sales came up the ranks with Bob and has always seen him as a threat. You think Bob is a good guy who has recently had some personal problems. If you believe your position regarding Bob is worth fighting for, then let's examine several ways this conversation might go when you address this situation with your boss.

In the first example, you've decided to go to the ends of the earth for this person. I'll let you decide if your efforts were worth the cost.

You: I understand that you wanted to talk to me about Bob.

Your boss: Yes, I did. The VP of sales isn't impressed with him and says he has to go. I want you to take care of this.

You: I think he's doing a decent job, and I'd like to keep him.

Your boss: Well, the decision isn't yours to make. Get rid of him and do so by Friday.

You: Can we at least discuss this?

Your boss: You're not hearing me. There's nothing to discuss. If you can't do it, I'll get someone who will.

In this scenario, you've misread the room. Your boss has made it quite clear in terms of what needs to happen next. When you asked, "Can we at least discuss this?" there was only one of two responses he could have given you. Unfortunately for you, he chose the answer you didn't want to hear. He took this one step further by expressing his doubt in your ability to carry out what he saw as a necessary management decision.

Here's another way to approach a conversation like this, where you can do what you think is ethically right and retain your standing with your boss.

You: Your message said you wanted to talk to me about Bob. I've been meaning to talk to you about him. Is now a good time?

Your boss: Sure, come in. Before you get going, I've got something you need to hear. The VP of sales is keen on getting rid of Bob. His sales are way behind everyone else's.

You: Yes, that's what I wanted to talk to you about. You're probably not aware that Bob's been going through some personal issues, which he seems to have recently resolved. Before all this happened, he was one of our top sales reps. If we fire him now, our biggest account may go with him.

Your boss: He's in charge of the C&C account?

You: Yes, his father-in-law is the founder and CEO of C&C. What if we did this instead? Give me a few months to work closely with him; I think we can get his sales numbers back to where they were. If at any time I find I'm wrong about this, I'll come immediately to you and let you know. Does that sound reasonable?

Your boss: Let's do this. I'll give you a chance to work with Bob, but at the same time, I want you to put some feelers out in case things don't work according to your plan. In the meantime, I'll tell the VP of sales that we've spoken and that we've got a plan to deal with this situation. If there's a problem, I'll let you know.

In the second example, you didn't ask for permission to speak, which is why you were able to plead your case. You also provided your boss with some critical information that she didn't know about. You offered up a reasonable solution and gave her something she could go back to the VP of sales with, that in all likelihood would have gotten him to back off.

Securing a Promotion

I can't think of a more political situation than the awarding of promotions. The leaders at the top can be found trying to move their favorites into a particular role, while the incumbents are jockeying for position. This scene plays out daily in organizations and is the plot for several movies, including the 2008 sleeper film *The Promotion*. It's one thing to watch a movie and laugh about it. It's another to personally experience the strife that occurs when you are in this situation. To help prepare you for what may come your way, let's look at two variations of a conversation on asking for a promotion.

The first scenario is when you feel you're entitled to this promotion.

You: When is it my turn for a promotion? I've been here six months longer than the person you just promoted.

Your boss: Promotions here are based on performance. What makes you think you're ready to move up?

You: Well, I've been here longer than anyone else on the team.

Your boss: I understand. However, seniority is not one of the factors we take into consideration when giving people more responsibility.

You: How long do you think I'm going to stay here doing the same job?

Your boss: That's not the question you should be asking me if you want a promotion. You should be asking what you need to do to get ready for a more strategic role in the company.

No one wants to give a promotion to someone who comes across as entitled, and they certainly won't give it to someone who threatens to leave.

Here's a script from someone who understands that promotions are based on performance, connections, and steering the conversation in the direction you want it to go. This approach requires courage and a dose of confidence.

You: Over the course of my employment, I have consistently offered out-of-the box ideas that have helped us expand our customer base and improve customer retention. I'd be remiss if I didn't remind you that I've developed a strong relationship with several managers who head up our key accounts. If this new opportunity went to me, I'd assimilate quite quickly into this role and would be able to offer additional value immediately.

Your boss: Well, that's true. However, another regional manager is pushing for your counterpart to assume this role.

You: I've been working on a couple of new initiatives regarding the customer experience. How about if you let me present this at next week's management meeting?

Your boss: That sounds like a good idea. This will allow you to showcase to others what I already know and could help me convince the director that you're the right person for this job.

The employee in this script approached the situation as a conversation and not a declaration. He guided his boss where he wanted to take him and now has the opportunity to convince the management team that he's by far the best candidate for this promotion.

Choosing Your Battles Wisely

Not every conversation is one worth having, which is why you want to be selective in terms of which battles to take on. Our time and energy are in limited supply and would be best spent in conversations where we're reasonably certain we can make a difference. I'm sharing with you four scenarios where you may want to skip the conversation and providing you with a list of questions to help you figure out if a conversation is worth having or skipping.

Here are some common scenarios where saying nothing may be the best thing.

You've Decided to Leave the Company

You've already mentally checked out of your job, and it's only a matter of time before your body follows suit. While in the short run it may feel good to get some things off your chest, in the long run, this move may do more harm than good. You've waited this long to say something—what's another few months?

The Situation Is Likely to Resolve Itself

Some situations will resolve on their own. For example, the division you work in is being sold off at the end of the month. You'll be remaining with company, while the person you've been meaning to speak with has been given an exit package. There's no longer a need to clear the air.

The Timing Is Wrong

You're incredibly disappointed with the paltry raise you received and planned to bring this up in your next one-to-one meeting with your boss. The company releases its earnings report the day before your meeting, and revenues are down considerably. Asking for more money right now will make you appear insensitive to what's going on in the company. Consider revisiting this conversation after you've made a significant contribution, such as saving the company a substantial amount of money, or when company earnings appear to be heading in the right direction.

The Person You're Speaking to Is Not Open to Change

I've personally dealt with a genuinely abusive boss. I quickly learned that no matter what I said, her behavior remained the same. If you're dealing with someone who is never going to change, then there is no need to subject yourself to another emotional episode where you leave the room dazed and confused and head straight to your office to call your therapist.

Here are some questions to help you decide if a conversation is worth having:

- Based on what I know about this person and our relationship, how likely is it that this conversation going to change anything?
- Do I have a secret agenda for this conversation? (e.g., revenge, getting someone fired, making myself look good at someone else's expense, etc.)
- Is this a problem that will resolve itself?
- Is this person open to feedback, or will I only be talking to hear myself speak?

- Am I open to hearing their side of the story?
- Do I have sensible solutions to offer?
- Am I the problem here and not them?

Taking Your Power Back: Having the Courage to Stand Up and Advocate for Yourself

How many times have you wanted to say something to someone but chose not to, and later wished you had stood up for yourself? Now and again, one of my coaching clients will describe a situation to me where they've regrettably allowed someone else to control their fate. They tell me that, at the time, they should have said something and ask me if there is any way to recover. It takes a heck of a lot of courage to stand up for yourself. The following is a story about a woman who stood her ground and persevered to overcome the odds. I hope you'll think of her the next time you find yourself trying to muster up the courage to have a political conversation that you're not sure you're ready to have.

In my early thirties, I joined the company (where I am currently employed) as an in-house lawyer. I was directly reporting to the president & CEO, a male in his late forties who is both eloquent and argumentative. Like in my other jobs and in other projects that I have handled, I put in all my efforts, and I worked ninety hours a week.

One year into the job, I knew that I would contribute more to the company and execute my vision more if were in a senior executive position, focusing more on the business side. I prepared a letter of intent for promotion and sent it via email to my boss, the PCEO. Our company policy requires that for promotions, the president and chief executive officer has to endorse the employee/applicant to the governing board (male-dominated) for an appointment. Hence, his endorsement was very crucial.

My boss was usually prompt in responding to emails, but days passed, and I didn't receive a response from him about my desire for a promotion. One day, after a client meeting, I asked if I could schedule an appointment with him to discuss my intent and to get a sense of his take on it.

I opened our meeting by saying, "I'd like to formally apply for the senior executive position that is currently available." He quickly dismissed my request by saying, "I don't see you as being the right fit for this position." He then stood up and began to walk to the door. I walked with him and followed him to the elevator and even to the parking area, requesting he give me a moment to hear my stance. It was a very awkward moment, but I knew that I needed to muster up the courage to have this conversation now, or the opportunity would go to someone else. I said, "In my brief tenure here, I've completed many successful projects and have been given additional responsibilities. I've more than proven that I am executive material."

Almost half an hour later, after a heated discussion with my contentious boss, he told me to see him in his office the next day.

I was worried. My thought was, am I fired?

Nervously, I went to his office the next day. After exchanging a few pleasantries, he said, "After much thought about our conversation in the elevator and the parking lot, I've changed my mind. I'm going to endorse you for the senior vice president position." To say I was relieved would be an understatement.

Months later, among hundreds of applicants for the position, I got the endorsement, the approval from the governing board, and the promotion. I'm now the officer-in-charge, president, and CEO of the company.

Aileen L. Amor-Bautista
Officer-in-Charge, President, and CEO
Credit Information Corporation

It took a great deal of fearlessness for Aileen to follow her boss to the parking lot so she could continue the conversation. After being told no, her willingness to persist goes to show the importance of living your life with no regrets.

Some of you may be thinking, "I could never do that. My personality type is the opposite of Aileen's." Perhaps you tend to let things roll off your back and then wish you hadn't. You're in good company. There are lots of people who will do anything not to rock the boat. However, what if your boat is about to sink because you're carrying way too much excess baggage? There is no reason to suffer in silence.

Here's what I tell my clients to do when they've reached the point where they realize their silence is costing them a great deal and is impacting their mental health. First, I have them select a conversation that is low risk. For example, maybe you're not thrilled with a coworker who can't seem to be bothered responding to your emails. You haven't said anything, and the problem persists. Or perhaps one of your peers tends to speak over you in meetings. In the beginning, you didn't think it was a big deal. However, now it's downright annoying. Next, I have them create a brief script of what they'd like to say to this person. I then have them practice their script and refine it, if need be. Finally, I have them schedule time to speak with this person and deliver their message. I always check back to see how things have gone. Usually, people tell me that the conversation went much better than expected.

In some cases, they'll tell me they have no idea of what they were worried about in the first place. I then ask them to select another conversation that they've been putting off and go through this process again. Most have plenty to choose from!

The mere act of standing up and advocating for yourself is life-changing for many. Too many people allow themselves to be pushed around. I remember hearing Oprah Winfrey say that the only way people can take advantage of you is if you let them. I remind myself of this often. You give away a tiny sliver of your power every time you allow someone to control you. Before you know it, you feel powerless. Now's the time to reset the bar and take your control back. You may not ace each of these conversations. That's okay. Keep in mind that failure is a stepping-stone to becoming a better version of you. And as my mentor Alan Weiss says, "If you're not failing, you're not trying!"

I've said this before, but it's worth repeating. Bravery comes in many different forms and is in the eye of the beholder. For some, being brave might be telling a superior they're wrong about a particular matter, while for others, it might be blowing the whistle on illegal activities going on inside their company. The only measurement that matters here is yours.

Here are some questions to help you determine your readiness to be courageous and say what's on your mind:

- If I don't speak up now, might I regret my decision later?
- Does a threat exist? If I avoid this conversation, might others get hurt?
- If I say something, will it make a difference?
- Am I giving away my power by not saying something?
- Am I being a people pleaser if I say nothing?
- Do the pros of speaking up outweigh the cons?
- What's the worst thing that can happen if I choose to push back?
- What might happen if I remain silent?
- What's holding me back from saying something, and is this a valid reason for remaining silent?

Conducting difficult workplace conversations will require some bravery. The more you practice, the more comfortable you'll be in handling situations that in the past you may have ignored. The goal here is to get to a place where you're able to say what needs to be said without hesitation.

The next chapter is our last, where we'll pull all these principles together and discuss where we go from here. You've come this far. Only one more chapter to go!

KEY LEARNING POINTS

- Courage is the determination to move forward despite the fear. It's more than a mindset or an emotion. It's a principle of action.
- The phrase "the courage of your talent" is a reminder that you are better than you think. Your superpowers will help you face your fears and say what needs to be said.
- The sooner you get comfortable with discomfort, the easier it will be for you to initiate a high-stakes conversation.

- Lots of people think that by *not* taking action, they'll be able to avoid discomfort. However, not taking action is a decision that can result in things remaining the same or worsening.

- Office politics is one game that is played in *every* organization. You can't ignore it, so you're best off getting good at dealing with highly charged conversations where office politics is present.

- Not every conversation is one worth having, which is why you want to be selective in terms of which battles to take on. Our time and energy is in limited supply and would be best spent in conversations where we're reasonably certain we can make a difference.

- It takes courage to stand up for yourself.

- You may choose not to have a conversation with someone for fear of rocking the boat. Do this one time too many and your boat may sink from the weight of your carrying too much excess baggage.

- Failure is a stepping-stone to becoming a better version of you.

08

Bringing It All Together

We've now arrived at the final chapter of the book. As you can see, there's a lot that goes into handling challenging work situations when your goal is to have a productive discussion *and* continue to build a relationship with the person you're addressing. You may have applied some of the techniques I've described along the way and had a conversation you were delaying. Things may have worked out better than planned, or maybe you weren't delighted with how things transpired. In this chapter, we'll be covering how to put the pieces together to ensure you improve how you handle high-stakes work conversations every time you have one. I'll share ideas on what to do next after having a difficult work conversation and how to move forward when it feels like you're in quicksand. I'll be discussing tips on creating a drama-free work environment so that difficult work conversations are the exception rather than the rule. We'll close out the chapter and the book with some encouraging words on why it's important to keep talking, even if doing so feels like the last thing you want to do.

Putting the Pieces Together

While writing this book, I worked on assembling a thousand-piece jigsaw puzzle with my family. While doing so, I realized many similarities between completing a jigsaw puzzle and preparing for and delivering difficult workplace conversations. Here's what I mean.

Before starting, we had a plan as to how we were going to solve this puzzle. We decided we'd assemble the frame first and sort similar-looking puzzle pieces into piles. We took turns building out different sections, as sometimes, with a fresh eye, one of us was able to see something the other one missed. We cheered each other on each time someone made a connection. The puzzle was more challenging than we anticipated, and there were many times when I wanted to throw in the towel. I mean, who takes on a 1,000-piece puzzle when the last one they assembled was 25 pieces?

You're in a great position to take on whatever conversation may come your way, or one that you've been avoiding, now that you've almost completed this book. However, here's a word of caution. As tempting as it may be to take on the most challenging situation first, which is the equivalent of doing a 1,000-piece jigsaw puzzle when you haven't successfully completed a 250-piece or 500-piece puzzle, don't. If you have a choice, choose a more manageable conversation. Give yourself time to practice these principles on conversations that aren't that complex and where the stakes aren't as high.

During your first few tough conversations, there's a good chance you'll make some mistakes and may say some things you regret. Should this occur, you'll more quickly recover from a lower-stakes conversation than one in which your career depends on getting the conversation right on your first attempt. The more you practice, the more comfortable you'll be addressing situations that you may have avoided in the past at all costs. You'll get to the point where you'll say what's on your mind to your boss, colleague, or direct report without even thinking, "This is going to be one of those tough conversations that I'm not looking forward to having."

As mentioned throughout this book, having a strategy to address a problematic work conversation is critical. Eventually, we may have solved the jigsaw puzzle without a plan. However, I'm reasonably sure that had we taken this approach, this darn puzzle would still be on my dining room table, and my family members would no longer be talking to me! Consider each of the seven principles of *Can We Talk?* to be one of the puzzle pieces needed to complete a difficult work conversation—meaning it doesn't matter which piece you connect first, as long as you eventually connect them all. With this in mind, it's okay to work on the second principle, which is clarity, before taking on confidence, which is the first principle. Or, if you realize that you lack credibility, which is principle number six, you may choose to work on changing the perception of those around you before thinking about compromise, which is principle number five.

Here's an example of how putting all the pieces together can lead to getting what you want and even more than you thought might be possible. An executive, whom I've come to know, shared a story with me about one of the most challenging workplace conversations of her career. She applied all the principles of *Can We Talk?* and ended up with pretty much what she wanted.

I wanted to leave a CEO role but wanted to go on a high note and with a severance package. As CEO, I had facilitated a merger with another organization and supported system integration to follow. I frankly did not enjoy working with my new boss. I wanted to take a break, and I wanted to do something else.

So, the tough conversation was broaching this topic with a boss with whom I did not have a strong relationship. Moreover, I had a solid and long relationship with my local board, which made my boss uncomfortable.

Before having such a conversation, I think it is important to define one's goals and leverage points. My goals were to:

1 Leave in a short time, maybe six weeks, as there is nothing worse than a lame duck.

2 Leave on a positive note with all the usual farewells, gifts, and accolades. This would be important for my next career step.

3 Receive the severance specified in my contract so that I could take some time to figure out my next role. This part was obviously a challenge.

I then examined my points of leverage:

1 I knew that my boss would be happier to have me gone because he felt like an outsider with my current board. And my board would want me treated very well after fourteen years.

2 I could point out system issues to my board and "stir the pot" for someone not entirely trusted by my board.

3 I sensed that my departure would make it easier to flatten the entire organization by shuffling positions across the system.

So, in approaching my boss, I designed the following questions:

1 Now that we are two years post-affiliation, I think that I am ready to do something else (after a well-deserved break). I wondered what you thought about that? You are so well connected in the industry. Would you help me find that next step?

2 I know that every health system is under tremendous financial pressure, and you are so financially astute. Would my departure assist you in gaining efficiencies in the top executive layer?

3 Given that my board remembers what I did for the organization, they are very loyal to me. Although I am voluntarily raising this possibility, I would think they would like to make sure I received my contractual severance and were able to honor my contributions at the usual events. I am sure they would want me to leave on a high note. This would certainly endear you to them and allow you to connect personally.

I went into that difficult conversation prepared and got everything I wanted. I could see in my boss's body language and tone that I hit all the right points. My intuition about what my boss needed was correct.

Anonymous

This meeting falls into the high-stakes category of difficult work conversations. CEO jobs are not easily found nor are CEO positions easy to fill. The CEO's boss had a lot on the line, in terms of how the board would view the loss of such a valuable employee. This executive could have approached her boss with a set of demands, which would have backfired in all likelihood. Instead, she approached the conversation as more of an exploration, and as a result was able to bring her boss along to her way of thinking. By doing so, she set the stage for a successful conversation. She entered the conversation with confidence and communicated clearly what she wanted to happen next. She was able to do this because she was clear on her objectives. She appealed to her boss's emotions by pointing out to her boss how much better off he'd be if she were to leave on a high note and how this move would enable her boss to establish a much-needed trusted relationship with the board, once she was out of the way. Her use of empathy and understanding provided her with the opportunity to offer up solutions that were in her boss's best interest. Throughout the conversation she remained curious, flexible, and asked her boss the right questions. Her thoughtful questions were not only questions—they were statements as well. She wasn't set on her terms and was willing to compromise, should she find herself in the position of having to do so. For example, she wanted to leave fairly soon. However, she was flexible and most likely would have agreed to stay until a replacement was found. Her boss wasn't keen on honoring her at all the usual events, since she was departing. However, he agreed, knowing that it was a small price to pay for a smooth exit and looking good in the eyes of the board. She had built up quite a bit of credibility with her boss and the board and had the courage of her talent to leave her current position, prior to finding a new role. She landed another CEO role quickly after departing and remains there today.

This story is an excellent example of managing a difficult conversation where the stakes are incredibly high and is a reminder that with careful preparation, the willingness to compromise, the proper delivery, and the courage of your convictions, anything *and* everything is possible.

Out of This World Difficult Work Conversations

I had the opportunity to interview NASA Astronaut Christina Koch, who currently holds the record for the longest continuous time in space by a woman and performed the first female team spacewalk. Christina had recently returned from spending a record-breaking 328 days in space when I had the opportunity to speak with her.

In particular, I wanted to find out if work conversations were much different in outer space than they are here on planet Earth. Christina confirmed what I suspected. Leadership challenges are *not* left behind when you leave the planet, including challenging work conversations. I asked Christina what it was like to be the "new gal in town" upon entry into the International Space Station. I especially wanted to know if she had gotten any pushback when leading a team of people who had been there for a while.

I asked if her fellow astronauts ever responded to a request she made with, "We've always done it this way," or "That's not how we do things here"? She chuckled and said, "Of course!" It was a relief to hear that leadership is pretty much the same no matter where you reside.

No doubt, as a leader, you're going to get some pushback from the people you manage. Having a prepared response such as, "I get that. However, we're going to try something new here," or "I understand. Let's try things this way, so we can see which approach works best" will serve you well.

There will be times that no matter what you do, it will feel next to impossible to change someone's mind. Should this happen to you, you'll have a decision to make. You'll need to decide if the situation is severe enough that you need to continue to proceed or if it's best to pause and reconvene when the conditions appear to be more in your favor. You may also decide this is not a battle worth fighting, in which case it's best to agree to disagree.

A client of mine shared a situation with me, where he needed to decide whether to tackle a conversation that he felt unprepared to address. One of his employees told him she was being sexually harassed by someone who happened to be on the list of people being laid off at the end of the month. My client had an easy way out. He could sweep this guy out of the organization under the guise of the upcoming reduction-in-force, or he could start an investigation, which he knew would be both disruptive and time-consuming. We discussed his dilemma, and eventually, he decided he would alert HR to the need for a full-fledged investigation. The next few days were tumultuous for all involved. Many uncomfortable conversations took place, and eventually, the decision was made to let this guy go. Despite having to go through this, my client told me that he was glad he decided to proceed. He knew he wouldn't be able to sleep at night, wondering if he had rewarded someone for bad behavior by giving them a generous reduction-in-force separation package on their way out the door. He also told me that the employee who came to him about this situation said she was extremely grateful that the company took sexual harassment matters seriously. She has reconfirmed her commitment to the organization and is willingly picking up the slack due to the recent downsizing that has occurred.

I applaud this client's decision to tackle what may be one of the most challenging work conversations any leader will ever have. If you've ever had to investigate a harassment claim, then you know what I mean. As the head of HR, I've conducted my share of sexual harassment investigations—one in particular sticks out in my mind. After attending an off-site sales conference, an employee filed a complaint with the VP of sales alleging that a coworker had sexually harassed her in his hotel room. The VP of sales, who was also a co-owner, went to his partner, the CEO, to tell him what had transpired. They both came to me and asked me to handle the investigation. They told me the goal was to ensure we did not lose the man accused of harassment, as he was a top performer.

I went into the meeting with the accuser thinking, "This is an impossible task. What if the investigation reveals she's telling the truth, and she wants this guy gone?" I met with the accuser, who shared her side of the story and listened intently to some very personal details that I wish I could forget. I then asked her the following question. "Ultimately, what would you like to see occur as a result of our conversation?" She said, "I don't want this guy fired. I just want the harassment to stop." Her response made it easier for me to take care of her needs while meeting the co-owners' goal. I then met with the accused, who shared intimate details with me (and I do mean intimate) of what had occurred. I sat there, doing my best not to look frazzled. In the end, things worked out fine, as we were able to honor the accuser's wish. However, a day doesn't go by when I don't think about what might have happened had she said, "I want this guy fired." Had that happened, I hope that the co-owners would have done the right thing since the accused admitted he had overstepped his bounds. If they hadn't, I would have had little choice but to resign.

Each of us has different lines in the sand that we're willing to cross—working in an environment where sales are more important than people didn't align with my values. Others may have taken a different position and may have remained, hoping they could change the culture. Not me. Culture starts at the top, and since I was never going to be an owner, I knew better than to try and change something that was not in my control to change.

What to Do Next after an Awkward Conversation

After the most challenging conversations, we generally breathe a sigh of relief and say, "Phew! Glad that's done! I hope I never have to have a conversation like that again." In my experience, rarely are these conversations one and done. They usually require follow-up. The question is, how? What can you say and do to make things less awkward and keep the conversation moving forward constructively?

I've spent almost my entire career helping leaders handle difficult work conversations and work collaboratively across the organization. I've seen firsthand the many benefits that occur when you follow up and work on building relationships long after the dust settles. Here are some critical steps that will help you rebuild a solid working relationship following some of the tougher conversations you may have.

Acknowledge the Awkwardness of the Conversation

Both parties may want to forget that a hard conversation ever took place—in reality, neither will, which is why you will want to acknowledge what transpired before deciding how to best proceed. I suggest you make it a point to follow up, even if you weren't the one who initiated the conversation. When doing so, make mention of the discomfort you both felt. Lastly, focus on the next steps you've both agreed upon to help you move forward. Here are some ice breakers you can use to start a follow-up conversation:

- Wow, that was a tough conversation, wasn't it?
- I don't know about you, but I'm glad we were able to clear the air.
- I imagine this was a pretty tough conversation to have. I'd like us to move past this.
- Thanks for your honesty. I'm not going to lie. It hurt to hear you say those things, but I know in the end I'll be better off as a result of knowing this.
- Thank you for having the courage to tell me what was on your mind. Where do we go from here?
- I'm grateful you took the time to allow me to process what you said. I've given our conversation considerable thought and have some ideas on what's required for us to work better as a team. Do you have a few minutes to discuss this?

Advance the Conversation

It's improbable that the awkward conversation you just had covered everything that had to be said. On the off chance it did, the other party may have been in shock and probably didn't fully comprehend everything that was said. As much as it may pain you, this is the time to summarize what's been said and agreed to and communicate the next steps to ensure your conversation has the results you've intended. You may do this in a follow-up email, or if you prefer, you can have this conversation in person. Should you choose the latter, be sure to summarize what's been said in a memo or email, so there is a record of what transpired. Documenting what was said helps create a path forward and builds a shared understanding of what both parties have agreed to, in order to work through the issue.

Here's what a follow-up email might look like for someone who has just had a conversation with an employee who is not performing up to standards:

This is a follow-up to the conversation we had on August 25th, where we discussed how your lack of follow-through is impacting team productivity and employee morale. We discussed three situations that occurred over the past several months, including the most recent incident, where your lack of follow-through resulted in the team missing the deadline to apply for a prestigious award that would have significantly enhanced our position in the marketplace.

You've agreed to the following: You'll immediately notify team members of any delay in agreed-upon timelines. If you feel you're being given more work than you're able to do, you'll come to me and tell me so that we can assess whether something should be reassigned. You will meet individually with your team members and apologize for your lack of follow-through. You'll seek their guidance in terms of what you need to do to rebuild trust.

You and I will meet again in one month's time to discuss your progress. We'll continue to work closely to ensure your performance remains on track.

Focus on Building Long-Lasting Relationships

Keep in mind that every interaction is two people talking to one another. If the only interaction you have with someone is negative, it won't be long before they avoid you altogether. Make it a point to go out of your way to have a positive conversation with someone you may have recently sparred with. This may be as simple as asking after a family member or complimenting them on something they said at a recent meeting. The key here is to be authentic. Saying you thought they did a great job of presenting at the executive conference when you thought they did a dismal job will do little to advance your relationship—that is, in the long run. Remember, there must be trust for a relationship to work, which won't be the case if the other person thinks you're saying things you don't mean. It's a good idea to involve the other person when trying to shape a more positive relationship. Here are some conversation starters to help you do this:

- I'm thinking we don't know each other all that well and that if we took the time to do so, we'd see that we have more in common than we think. Are you free to grab a sandwich this week or next?

- We are both working toward a common goal of making this company number one in the marketplace, right? (Emphasize the "we" here.) I found an article that I thought you'd enjoy reading. This piece includes an excellent synopsis of some of the challenges our industry will be facing in the coming year. With your permission, I'd like to send you a copy.

- I couldn't help but overhear in our meeting that your son is applying to the same college that my son attends. If you'd like, I'd be happy to see if my son would be open to having a conversation with your child about campus life.

Actively building positive relationships, especially if you don't particularly care for someone's personality, is not easy. However, building relationships at work must be done and will get more comfortable with practice. It's also important to keep in mind that it takes two people to have a relationship. Even though you may feel it's your boss or coworker's responsibility to move the relationship forward, this may not always happen. Therefore, you need to be prepared to take the torch and carry it across the finish line. Don't make the rookie mistake of assuming no news is good news. The other party may get busy, which is why you may have to take the lead, even when it feels like this role should be shouldered by someone else. In the end, you may not wind up breaking bread together. However, chances are reasonably good that you'll remain civil to one another as you work toward a shared goal, and who knows, you may actually wind up liking one another.

Creating a Drama-Free Work Environment

Have you noticed how some workplaces have more drama than others? I have. Drama manifests in various workplace ways, including insubordination, backstabbing, office gossip, finger-pointing, power struggles, and how people relate to one another in the office.

What's interesting to me is that high-drama workplaces aren't limited to specific industries. For example, I have two clients in the same industry. One client rarely has a situation that requires immediate intervention and an uncomfortable conversation, whereas the other client seems always to have something brewing. You may be wondering how can this be? Don't companies in the same industry hire similar people? Yes; however, who you hire and how you choose to manage people matters considerably.

In my many years of consulting, I have seen the impact company culture has on everything that transpires both inside and outside the organization. I'm defining company culture here as a set of shared values and beliefs. As I stated earlier, company culture is set by those at the top of the organization. It's the underpinning for company policies, including how people are managed and how they interact with one another. When the CEO and his or her management team set a particular standard, others follow suit. For example, my client company's CEO, with a drama-free workplace, is a direct communicator. He doesn't mince words. If there's a problem, he'll let you know.

In contrast, the CEO of the other company is more of a people pleaser. He doesn't like confrontation and wants to be liked by everyone he meets. As a result, critical issues that should be addressed lie dormant until they reach a point where they implode. The conversations that follow these implosions are more challenging than those that would have taken place had the issue been handled from the start.

Some of you may be thinking, "Well, the company I work for is definitely more prone to drama than most. Since I'm not at the top, there's nothing I can do about this. I guess I'm just going to have to get really good at facilitating high-stakes conversations since I'll be continuing to have a lot of them." That's not necessarily true. Every company has subcultures, which may explain why it may appear sunny in sales and pouring rain in customer service. All you have to do is go onto a site like Glassdoor, where employees share what's it's like to work for a particular organization, and you can see what I mean. You've got some people touting a particular workplace while others are warning people to stay away. If you take a closer look, you'll see that frequently the reviewers work in different departments.

Here's what subcultures mean for those of you who are leading workgroups. You can create the subculture of your liking—one that is drama-free. Start by modeling the behavior you'd like others to follow. For example, let's say you have an employee who is not pulling his weight. Do what you'd expect one of your supervisors in a similar situation to do—speak to this employee about his performance when you notice there is a problem. Or, perhaps you looked the other way when you heard about elevated levels of office gossip. In retrospect, you realize now that doing so was a mistake, as things seem to have gotten out of hand. It's not too late to take control and reset the bar. Pull the team together and say something like, "I've recently noticed that there's been a lot of gossiping going on around here. This kind of behavior can be hurtful and is unwelcome here. I'm putting everyone on notice that if you are involved in fanning the rumor mills, you will face disciplinary action, up to and including termination." Then be prepared to immediately speak with anyone who continues to behave in this manner.

Lack of clarity can also create office drama. Let's say you've assigned a project to several people on your team. You weren't specific in terms of who was responsible for what. One team member seems to feel he's carrying the lion's share of the work and has made sure everyone around him knows this. You could have avoided this situation had you been specific in terms of work division. You'll need to have a conversation with both parties to ensure things get back on track. However, before doing this, you need to clarify who is responsible for each phase of the project. After doing so, arrange for a call or meeting with the employee who feels he's doing most of the work and say something like, "I understand you feel that the responsibility for this project has pretty much fallen on your shoulders. Is my understanding correct?" Let's assume the person says yes since he's admitted this to anyone and everyone who would listen. You can then say, "I can understand why you might feel this way. When I assigned the project to you and Tom, I failed to specify my expectations. For that, I apologize. I intended for you to work directly with the client to define the specifications needed to build the new product. Tom will then take these specs and establish a supply chain to ensure we can get the product built to our client's specifications and within budget. I'll be meeting with Tom later today to ensure he's aware of his role in this project." In the future, be sure people have a clear understanding of their responsibilities as well as your expectations. By doing so, you'll avoid the office drama that occurs when people are jockeying for position or when someone feels they're also doing someone else's job.

One of the most challenging workplace dramas occurs when two people who work for you see things in a completely different way. In situations like this, you'll need to facilitate what will most likely be an emotionally charged conversation. Think of yourself as the mediator. You'll still follow the seven principles outlined in this book, only your role in the discussion will be different. You won't be leading the conversation. Instead, you'll be providing direction and encouragement to both parties and working collaboratively with them to find a mutually satisfying solution. Here's a situation where I had to intervene and mediate a conversation between two of my employees, causing a lot of workplace drama.

Beth had worked for me for several years when Lisa arrived on the scene. Beth was a steady worker who took pride in arriving on time and being ready to start her workday promptly at 8:30 a.m. Lisa, on the other hand, was more of a free spirit. Sometimes she'd be at her desk ready to begin her workday on time, and other days she could be found in the lunchroom chatting while grabbing a coffee. Soon after Lisa's arrival, it became apparent to everyone around them that the two of them were having a difficult time working together. When their rift began to impact others in the department, I decided an intervention was necessary. I called them both into my office, and here's how the conversation transpired.

Me: I couldn't help but notice there's tension between the two of you, which is impacting the rest of the department. I thought it was best for all of us to meet, to see if we can reconcile whatever may be going on. Beth, do you want to go first?

Beth: Sure. I guess I know that we have to cover the receptionist's phones until 9:00 a.m., which means one of us has to be at our desk promptly at 8:30 a.m. to open the phone lines. It feels like I'm the only one that is adhering to the rules. On mornings where one of my kids isn't feeling well, I feel particularly stressed, as I can't rely on Lisa to assume this task. She's late more than she is on time.

Me: We're on different floors, so I haven't noticed this. Lisa, what's your take on what's going on?

Lisa: I'm here on time every day. Just ask anyone who goes to the lunchroom early in the morning, as the first thing I do when I arrive is stop there for a cup of coffee. I don't see what the problem is here, although I do sense a less than friendly attitude from Beth.

Me: Lisa, I know when I hired you, we spoke about the need to be at your desk, ready to work, every day at 8:30 a.m. Has something changed at home that is preventing you from doing this? Can you see why Beth feels the way she does?

Lisa: Well, yes. My stepson is now living with us two days a week, and I'm responsible for making sure he gets to school on time. He's with us on Mondays and Tuesdays. Some days traffic is heavier than others, and our mornings are so hectic that I don't even have time to grab a cup of coffee before leaving.

Beth: I didn't know your stepson was living with you now. I know how stressful it can be to get a teenager off to school on time.

Me: Yes, it certainly can be difficult balancing work and family. What can be done here to make things easier for both of you?

Beth: Well, what if you changed my work hours to 8:00 a.m., which would allow me to leave here promptly at 5:00 p.m.? I'll take complete responsibility for the phones. Lisa could continue to work 8:30 a.m. to 5:30 p.m.

Lisa: I start a night class next month that meets twice a week. The class starts at 6:00 p.m. Luckily, those are the days when my stepson isn't with us. It would be great if I could leave at 5:00 p.m. a few days a week. How about this? What if Beth were scheduled to work 8:00 a.m. to 5:00 p.m. on Monday, Tuesday, and Wednesday, and I committed to that schedule on Thursday and Friday?

Beth: I could live with that.

Me: Just so we're clear here, when I say be ready to start your workday, that means being at your desk, with coffee in hand, at your official start time. Is that understood?

Lisa: Yes.

To ensure a successful outcome, I followed many of the seven principles outlined in this book. I began the conversation by practicing clarity. I was clear on my objective before facilitating the discussion. I needed to be sure the phones were covered from 8:30 a.m. to 9:00 a.m., and I wanted both parties to figure out a solution that would satisfy them both. I was their boss, so of course, I could have told them exactly what they each needed to do. However, had I done so, I may have gotten compliance, which is way less effective than commitment. Having them come up with their own plan increased the chances of sustainable results, a better working relationship between them, and harmony in the department. I showed empathy, as did Beth when acknowledging the challenge of balancing work and family life, and I came across as curious when I asked what could be done to make things easier for both of them. I sought to bring them to a place of compromise, which I could do when both parties came up with a workable solution. As a side note, I'm told Beth and Lisa are now the best of friends.

Staying on Track

I've conducted enough tough conversations to know that there will be times that people will try to pull you off track. You'll be conversing with someone, thinking, "Hey, this is going pretty well," when

BRINGING IT ALL TOGETHER

suddenly you hit a roadblock. How you react will determine whether you're able to continue the conversation and achieve a positive result. With that in mind, here are some of the more common blockers that people will put up along the way and how to plow through them.

"That's not how we do things around here."

It's common knowledge that many people don't do well with change. Knowing this, here's how to respond when someone says this to you. "I understand this approach may be different than what you're used to doing. For now, let's try it this way, and we can reconvene to discuss how things are working."

"Well, X does this too. Are you going to be having this same conversation with them?"

I consider this to be a deflection move. The person you're speaking with is doing their best to move the attention from them to someone else. Here's how I would respond. "I'm not here to discuss X. I'm here to talk with you about…"

"Why are you picking on me?"

When faced with a difficult conversation, it's not uncommon for people to feel like they're being singled out. When this occurs, you could say something like, "Why do you feel I'm picking on you?" Most likely, they'll then argue that someone else has been doing the same thing, at which point you can refer to the response I've provided above.

"I'm offended by what you just said. How dare you speak to me this way!"

Before going further, stop and think about what you just said. How was your tone when delivering the message? Did you choose your words wisely? There are two paths you can go down. If your tone and your words were way off, you could respond by saying, "You know, you're right. I'm sorry I offended you. That wasn't my intent. With your permission, let me rephrase this." If you believe the way you delivered your message was on point, then say, "I'm sorry you feel this way. However, it's important that you understand the seriousness of the matter. I'd be remiss if I sugarcoated this. Let's focus on the facts and what needs to happen next."

And then there is the moment when there are no words—only sniffles or tears. That's a showstopper for most. When this occurs, take a deep breath and then suggest a pause. Say, "It looks like you could use a few minutes to compose yourself." Then wait until you feel they've calmed down and try to continue the conversation. If the person you're speaking with still appears to be upset, end the meeting by saying, "Let's schedule a date and time to reconvene." Then schedule the follow-up meeting before the person leaves your office or disconnects from the call.

Keep Talking

Throughout this book, I've emphasized the need to keep talking, as rarely is a difficult conversation a one and only sort of thing. If there is someone in particular that you butt heads with, you're usually going to clash more than once. If you've hired or inherited a challenging employee, this person isn't going to become someone who can easily be managed after one conversation. Should you find yourself losing hope, consider the following.

Work on Shifting your Relationship from One of Opposition to a Partnership

It's easy to see your conversational partner as your opponent in the middle of a difficult conversation. Try repositioning yourself—both mentally and physically—to be side by side with the other person so that you're focused on resolving the same problem. For example, maybe you sense your boss is getting frustrated with you because you keep missing deadlines. You're doing all you can to get your reports done on time. However, severe flaws in the software system make this next to impossible. Up until now, you may have viewed your boss as enemy number one. He's not. He's getting heat from his boss concerning missed deadlines.

Here's a way you can shift the conversation to one of a partnership. You can say to your boss, "I get the sense you think I don't care about deadlines since I've missed a few. This couldn't be further than the truth. If you have a moment, I'd like to explain some systems issues that I've observed and a few ideas I have for doing reports more efficiently."

Reframe Your Conversation from Convincing to Learning

Conversations often go off the rails when we try to convince someone of our point of view, especially when we haven't taken the time to understand where they're coming from. Earlier in this book, I told you about my brother Mark, who, shall we say, is passionate about his political beliefs. In the past, I've tried to convince him to see things from my perspective. Rarely does that work (okay, it's never worked). However, we can have a productive conversation when I approach the conversation as someone interested in learning more about his point of view. I start most conversations off with him by saying, "Help me to understand." I say this because I really do want to learn why he feels a particular way. Consciously shifting into a learning mode will help you gain the insight needed to be resourceful, collaborate, and move the conversation forward. Loosen your grip on your own viewpoint, at least temporarily, so you can make space to take in someone else's point of view. Who knows, you may even wind up changing your mind!

Speak Your Truth

Put your intentions on the table for all to see. People are often overly worried about offending someone, so instead, they are less than truthful. Or they say just about everything, except what needs to be said. This leaves the other person guessing in terms of what was really meant. I know there have been plenty of times when someone has said to me, "Can we talk?" I agree to do so, and when they tell me why they wanted to speak with me, I often leave puzzled. Has this happened to you as well? If you encounter a situation like this, you might say, "I'm a tad confused. Why don't you tell me exactly what's on your mind?" To avoid doing the same to someone else, begin the conversation by clearly stating your intention. "I'd like each of us to get our concerns on the table to ensure we don't miss anything. Do you prefer to go first, or should I?"

Constructively Deconstructing Assumptions

Ask someone what's getting in the way of building a solid relationship with someone at work, and they'll likely describe what they believe was in the other person's mind. They'll say things like, "They want my job and will do anything to get it" or "He's waiting for me to fail." The assumptions we make about other people may reflect more about ourselves than what the other person has on their mind. I've said it before. However, it bears repeating. We can't possibly know what someone else is thinking unless we ask. If we say nothing and continue to operate using our assumptions, we'll never arrive at our intended destination, which is ultimately having a productive conversation where both parties feel understood.

Acknowledge Where You May Have Gone Wrong

Nothing will help to move a stuck conversation along faster than a sincere apology. The keyword here is sincere. An apology that is not heartfelt will do more harm than good. Acknowledging where you might have gone wrong demonstrates you're human and may encourage the other person to do the same. Here are a few examples of how you can get the conversation rolling again. "I can see where I may have given you the impression that I'm jockeying for your position. That's not at all my intent, and if I made you feel that way, I'm truly sorry. My enthusiasm to help us achieve stellar results this year may have been a bit much." Or you could say, "I feel like we've gotten off on the wrong foot. I take responsibility for that. Can we start over?"

As you put into practice what you've learned in this book, you'll find that it will get easier to have an open and honest conversation at work. You can also apply these same principles at home and improve your personal relationships as well. I encourage you to keep this book close by and refer back to it when you need a refresher. If you have a question or would simply like to talk, feel free to reach out to me at Roberta@robertamatuson.com.

As you progress through your career, you'll go through a lot of changes. However, one thing that will never change is the need to communicate effectively. You have the tools you need to handle whatever tough conversation may come your way. Go forth confidently and remember—keep talking!

INDEX

CPSIA information can be obtained
at www.ICGtesting.com
Printed in the USA
JSHW012355270821
18267JS00010B/260

9 781398 601307